THE
ZIMBABWE
STUDENT'S
HANDBOOK

THE ZIMBABWE STUDENT'S HANDBOOK

ACADEMIC BOOKS

HARARE

Published by Academic Books (Pvt.) Ltd.
P.O. Box 567, Harare, Zimbabwe.

© Academic Books (Pvt.) Ltd., 1989.

The Zimbabwe Student's Handbook was compiled by
Kay Sayce assisted by Bruce Brine, Roy Guthrie, Hugh Lewin,
Langton Mavudzi, Barbara Murray, Andre Proctor, Irene Staunton
and Roger Stringer. The publishers wish to record their appreciation
for helpful advice given by the Department of National Parks,
the Department of Culture, Staff of the Queen Victoria Museum and
the Curriculum Development Unit of the Ministry of Primary
and Secondary Education, Harare.

Cover design: Stewart Paterson.

Maps: Lorraine Mons.

Typesetting: Irene MacLeod.

Printed by Mazongororo Paper Converters (Pvt.) Ltd., Harare.

ISBN 0 949229 12 1

CONTENTS

CONTENTS

PROVINCES AND MAIN TOWNS

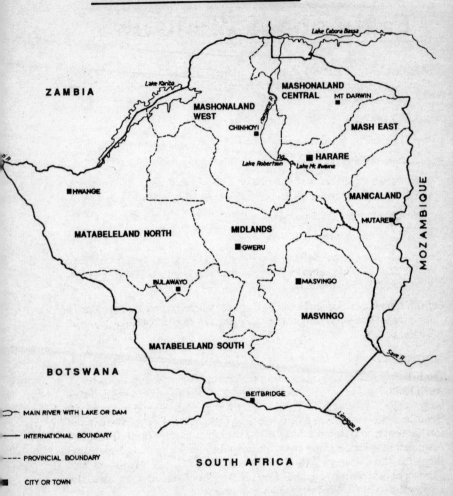

ZAMBIA

Lake Cabora Bassa

Lake Kariba

MASHONALAND
CENTRAL MT DARWIN

MASHONALAND
WEST

CHINHOYI

MASH EAST

HARARE

Lake Robertson Lake Mt Rwaine

HWANGE

MANICALAND

MUTARE

MOZAMBIQUE

MATABELELAND NORTH

MIDLANDS

GWERU

BULAWAYO

MASVINGO

MASVINGO

MATABELELAND SOUTH

Save R

BOTSWANA

BEITBRIDGE

Limpopo R

⌐ MAIN RIVER WITH LAKE OR DAM

── INTERNATIONAL BOUNDARY

---- PROVINCIAL BOUNDARY

■ CITY OR TOWN

SOUTH AFRICA

PART ONE

Facts about Zimbabwe

The Republic of Zimbabwe lies in southern Africa, between 25°E and 34°E, and 15°S and 23°S. It is bordered by Zambia, Mozambique, South Africa and Botswana.

Area: 391 000 sq km

Cities: Harare (capital city); Bulawayo; Gweru; Mutare

Population: 7 501 470 at the 1982 census; 1988 estimate 8 400 000

People: African 94% (of which 67% are Shona-speaking, 15% Ndebele-speaking); Non-African (European, Asian and other) 6%

Population density: 25,5 persons per sq km

Population growth rate: 3,14% per annum

Currency: Zimbabwe dollar, divided into 100 cents. Notes in units of $2, $5, $10, $20; coins in denominations of 1 cent, 5 cents, 10 cents, 20 cents, 50 cents and $1

Official languages: Shona, Ndebele, English; officially recognized minority languages: Kalanga, Tonga, Venda, Shangaan, Sotho, Nambya, Nyanja/Cewa, Sotho

GOVERNMENT

Zimbabwe is a sovereign republic, which attained Independence on 18 April 1980. The Head of State is the Executive President. The legislative body is Parliament, which consists of the Senate (made up of 40 Senators) and the House of Assembly (made up of 100 Members of Parliament), to become a single 150 member Assembly in 1990. The responsibility for deciding government policy and preparing legislation lies with the Cabinet. The Cabinet consists of Senior Ministers and Ministers appointed by the President. The President is also the Commander-in-Chief of the Defence Forces.

President: His Excellency Robert Gabriel Mugabe

Vice-President: The Hon. Simon Vengayi Muzenda M.P.;

Senior Ministers: Dr. The Hon. Bernard Thomas Chidzero M.P.; The Hon. Joshua Mqabuko Nkomo M.P.

Ministries: Community and Co-operative Development and Women's Affairs; Defence; Energy and Water Resources and Development; Finance, Economic Planning and Development; Foreign Affairs; Health; Higher Education; Home Affairs; Industry and Technology; Information, Posts and Telecommunications; Justice, Legal and

IMPORTANT AGRICULTURAL PRODUCTS

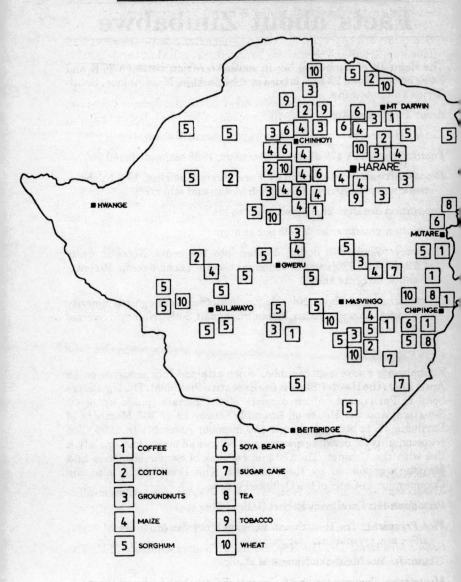

1	COFFEE	6	SOYA BEANS
2	COTTON	7	SUGAR CANE
3	GROUNDNUTS	8	TEA
4	MAIZE	9	TOBACCO
5	SORGHUM	10	WHEAT

Parliamentary Affairs; Labour, Manpower Planning and Social Welfare; Lands, Agriculture and Rural Resettlement; Local Government, Rural and Urban Development; Mines; Natural Resources and Tourism; National Security; National Supplies; Political Affairs; Primary and Secondary Education; Public Service; Public Construction and National Housing; Trade and Commerce; Transport; Youth, Sport and Culture. In addition, there are four Ministers of State for Political Affairs and one Minister of State for National Scholarships.

Defence Forces: Zimbabwe National Army (ZNA); Air Force of Zimbabwe (AFZ); Zimbabwe People's Militia (ZPM); Zimbabwe Republic Police (ZRP).

PROVINCES

Zimbabwe is divided into eight administrative Provinces. Each province is headed by a Provincial Governor, who represents the government and is automatically a member of the Senate. The eight provinces are as follows together with the Provincial Governors as of December 1989:

Matabeleland North – Zwelibanzi Muzilethi
Matabeleland South – Mark Dube
Mashonaland Central – Joseph Kaparadza
Mashonaland East – Rwizi Ziyenge
Mashonaland West – Mudhomeni Chivende
Midlands – Tranos Makombe
Masvingo – Dzikamai Mavhaire
Manicaland – Bishop Joshua Dhube

NATIONAL HOLIDAYS

Independence Day	18 April
Workers' Day	1 May
Africa Day	25 May
Heroes' Day	11 August
Armed Forces' Day	12 August

ECONOMY

The economy of Zimbabwe is based mainly on agriculture, the manufacturing industry and mining.

Major crops: Maize, tobacco, cotton, wheat, soyabeans, oilseeds, sugar, coffee, tea, groundnuts, sorghum.

Livestock: Beef cattle, dairy cattle, sheep.

Major manufactured products: Foodstuffs, drink and tobacco, textiles, clothing and footwear, chemical and petroleum products, metal and metal products.

Major minerals: Gold, asbestos, chromium, antimony, coal, copper, nickel, iron ore, silver, tin, lithium, cobalt.

IMPORTANT MINERAL PRODUCTS

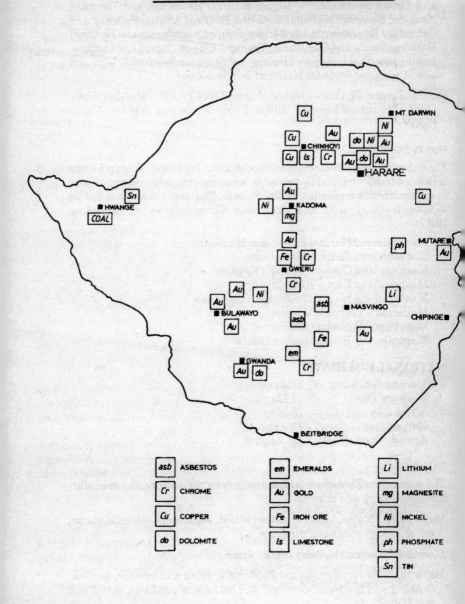

asb	ASBESTOS	em	EMERALDS	Li	LITHIUM
Cr	CHROME	Au	GOLD	mg	MAGNESITE
Cu	COPPER	Fe	IRON ORE	Ni	NICKEL
do	DOLOMITE	ls	LIMESTONE	ph	PHOSPHATE
				Sn	TIN

Zimbabwe's exports consist mainly of raw materials, while its imports consist mainly of manufactured items.

Main exports: Tobacco, ferrochrome, cotton, asbestos, iron and steel, nickel, sugar, coffee, copper and manufactured goods.

Main imports: Petroleum products, telecommunications equipment, machinery transport equipment, aircraft and spares, wheat, textile piece goods, industrial tools and hardware, motor vehicles and power machines.

TRANSPORT

Air: The national airline is Air Zimbabwe. Air Zimbabwe operates local, regional and international cargo and passenger services. An international cargo service is operated by Affretair.

Rail: The railway network is administered by the National Railways of Zimbabwe. The railway lines link Zimbabwe to Mozambique, Botswana, South Africa and Zambia.

Road: Road transport is made up mainly of private motor vehicles, light commercial vehicles and trucks. Road haulage is an important means of commercial transport. Public road transport is provided by urban and rural bus services.

Major bridges: The major bridges are Alfred Beit Bridge (over Limpopo River), Birchenough Bridge (over Save River), Otto Beit Bridge (over Zambezi River) and Victoria Falls Bridge (over Zambezi River).

NATIONAL FLAG

The flag of Zimbabwe is made up of seven horizontal bands of colour which are (from top to bottom) green, yellow, red, black, red, yellow, green.

The green bands symbolize Zimbabwe's agriculture; the yellow bands symbolize Zimbabwe's mineral wealth; the red bands symbolize the blood spilled during the liberation war; and the black band symbolizes the black majority of the people.

On the left of the flag is a white triangle, in which there is a yellow Zimbabwe Bird on a red five-pointed star. The white triangle symbolizes peace. The Zimbabwe Bird is the national emblem. The red star symbolizes the nation's aspirations.

NATIONAL EMBLEMS

The national emblem of Zimbabwe is the Zimbabwe Bird. Six soapstone carvings of a bird were found in the Eastern Enclosure of the Hill Complex at the national monument, Great Zimbabwe. They were taken to South Africa by white travellers in the 1890s, but after Independence they were returned to Zimbabwe and are now housed in the site museum at Great Zimbabwe.

The national flower of Zimbabwe is the flame lily, (jongwe, amakhulume, *Gloriosa superba*).

NATIONAL PARKS

MANA POOLS
SAPI
DANDE
CHEWORE
HURUNGWE
DOMA
SIBILOBILO
CHARARA
TINGWA RAPHIA PALM
LAKE KARIBA
NYAMANYETSI
MT. DARWIN
MATUSADONA
MAWARI RAPHIA PALM
UMFURUDZI
ISLAND 52?
CHETE
CHINHOYI
CHIZARIRA
CHINHOYI CAVES
MAZOWE
CHIBWATATA
ROBERTSON
NATIONAL
EWANRIGG
ZAMBEZI
CHIRISA
DUMFULI
HARARE
KAVIRA
HARTLEY
McILWAINE
VICTORIA FALLS
NYANGA
HWANGE
RUSAPE
DEKA
MAIN CAMP
MBAZE PAN
NGEZI
MUTARE
HWANGE
SEBAKWE ACACIA KAROO
SEBAKWE
BUNGA FOREST
VUMBA
SEBAKWE GREAT DYKE
SEBAKWE MOUNTAIN ACACIA
VUMBA
GWERU
CHIMANIMANI
CHIMANIMANI ELAND
BULAWAYO
MUSHANDIKE
MASVINGO
RUSITU FOREST
TSHABALALA
LAKE CUNNINGHAM
KYLE
CHIPINGE HARONI FOREST
CHIPINGE
UMZINGWANI
MATOPOS
MANJIRENJI
BANGALA
GWANDA
CHISEKERA HOT SPRINGS
PIONEER
TOLO
MALAPATI
GONA RE ZHOU
TULI
SOUTH CAMP
MANJINJI PAN
BEITBRIDGE

○ BOTANICAL GARDEN

☐ BOTANICAL RESERVE

▨ NATIONAL PARK

▥ RECREATIONAL PARK

▥ SAFARI AREA

▨ SANCTUARY

HISTORICAL SITES

There are many thousands of historical sites in Zimbabwe, ranging from Stone Age sites, such as the numerous rock art caves and rock engravings, to Iron Age sites, such as Great Zimbabwe and Kame. There are also many historical monuments in Zimbabwe, the most important one being Heroes' Acre, near Harare.

Stone Age: 1266 sites plus 3517 rock painting sites (recorded to date). The major ones are Amadzimba Cave (Matopos Communal Land), Nyazonga Rock Shelter (Mutasa North Communal Land), Dombozanga Rock Shelter (Mtetengwe Communal Land), Pomongwe Cave (Matopos National Park), Bambata Cave (Matopos National Park), Diana's Vow Cave (Rusape), Cave of Hands (Mchela Hill, Gwanda District), Nswatugi Cave (Matopos National Park), Tshangula Cave Matopos National Park), Zombepata Cave (Guruve Communal Land), White Rhino Shelter (Matopos National Park) and Silozwane Cave (Matopos National Park).

Iron Age: 3029 recorded sites. The major ones are Great Zimbabwe, Kame, Naletale, Danangombe and the ruins in the Nyanga area.

Modern: Heroes' Acre, outside Harare, the burial place of Zimbabwe's national heroes. There are also provincial and district Heroes' Acres. An important site is the Battle of Chinhoyi Memorial, near Chinhoyi.

NATIONAL PARKS

About five million hectares of Zimbabwe's land area are set aside for the conservation of plants and animals. The main national parks, recreational parks, safari areas, botanical reserves and sanctuaries are listed below:

National Parks:

Chimanimani (17 110 ha)	Matopos (42 400 ha)
Chizarira (191 000 ha)	Matusadona (140 700 ha)
Gona-re-zhou (505 300 ha)	Nyanga (33 000 ha)
Hwangwe (1 465 100 ha)	Victoria Falls (2 340 ha)
Kazuma Pan (31 300)	Zambezi (56 010 ha)
Mana Pools (219 600 ha)	

Botanical Reserves:

Bunga Forest (495 ha)	Sebakwe Acacia Karoo (60 ha)
Chisekera Hot Springs (95 ha)	Sebakwe Great Dyke (165 ha)
Haroni Forest (20 ha)	Sebakwe Mountain Acacia (53 ha)
Mawari Raphia Palm (34 ha)	South Camp (26 ha)
Mazowe (46)	Tingwa Raphia Palm (290 ha)
Pioneer (38 ha)	Tolo River (44 ha)
Rusitu Forest (150 ha)	Vumba (42 ha)

Botanical Gardens:

Ewanrigg (286 ha)	Vumba (200 ha)
National Botanic (67 ha)	

Sanctuaries:
Chimanimani (1 800 ha)
Pan (300 ha)
Mbaze Pan (40 ha)

Mushandike (12 900 ha) Manjinji
Nyamanyetsi (2 480 ha)
Tshabalala (1 100 ha)

Safari Areas:
Charara (169 200 ha)
Chete (108 000 ha)
Chewore (339 000 ha)
Chipinge (26 100 ha)
Chirisa (171 300 ha)
Dande (52 300 ha)
Deka (51 000 ha)
Doma (94 500 ha)
Umfurudzi (76 000 ha)

Hartley 'A' (44 500 ha)
Hurungwe (289 400 ha)
Island 52 (4 ha)
Malapati (15 400 ha)
Matetsi (295 500 ha)
Sapi (118 000 ha)
Sibilobilo (4 400 ha)
Tuli (41 600 ha)

Recreational Parks:
Bangala (2 700ha)
Chibwatata (10 ha)
Chinhoyi Caves (120 ha)
Kavira (50 ha)
Kyle (16 900 ha)
Lake Cunningham (4 172 ha)
Lake Kariba (287 200 ha)
Lake Matopos (2 900 ha)

Lake Robertson (11 200 ha)
Manjirenji (3 400 ha)
Ngezi (5 800 ha)
Robert McIlwaine (6 180 ha)
Sebakwe (2 600 ha)
Umfuli (12 700 ha)
Umzingwane (1 233 ha)

Certains animals in Zimbabwe have special protection. This means that by law they cannot be hunted or killed without special permission from the Minister of Natural Resources. All these species are known as Specially Protected Species.

Mammals: aardwolf, bat-eared fox, brown hyena, cheetah, gemsbok, Lichtenstein's hartebeest, pangolin, black rhinoceros, white rhinoceros, wild dog, roan antelope.

Reptiles: python.

Birds: African fish eagle, African hawk eagle, Ayre's hawk eagle, bateleur eagle, black eagle, black-breasted snake eagle, black sparrowhawk, brown snake eagle, blue swallow, all bustards and korhaans, all cranes, crowned eagle, fish eagle, all flamingoes, hamerkop, lanner falcon, long-crested eagle, martial eagle, osprey, all pelicans, peregrine falcon, secretary bird, all storks, taita falcon, tawny eagle, all vultures.

Plants: Among the specially protected plants are aloes, orchids, flame lily, borassus palm, cycads, mangrove fern, mutuputupu tree, raphia palm, Rhunde star, Save star, staghorn fern, Warburgia and tree ferns.
Many of these plants are very rare and only found in isolated areas of Zimbabwe. Conservationists, however, stress the absolute importance

of maintaining the balance of nature which the random destruction of any plant or animal life can destroy.

GEOGRAPHY
More than half of Zimbabwe is above 1 000m above sea level. The land can be divided into the highveld, which runs through the centre of the country; the lowveld regions of the Zambezi and Limpopo areas; and the eastern highlands.

The main vegetation areas are: highveld – moist savanna woodland and dry savanna woodland; lowveld – grassland and savanna woodland; eastern highlands – moist savanna woodland and forest.

Highest point: Mount Inyangani, 2 592m

Lowest point: Confluence of Save and Runde Rivers, 250m

Major rivers: Zambezi, Limpopo, Save, Runde, Manyame

Highest waterfall: Mtarazi Falls, 762m

Widest Waterfall: Victoria Falls, 1 708m

Largest lakes / dams: Kariba (on Zambezi River) 180 600 million cubic metres; Kyle (on Mutirikwe River) 1 425 million cubic metres; Darwendale (on Manyame River) 490 million cubic metres; Mazwikadei (on Mukwadzi River) 360 million cubic metres; Manyuchi (on Mwenezi River) 320 million cubic metres

ABBREVIATIONS IN COMMON USE
AAZ	Automobile Association of Zimbabwe
AFC	Agricultural Finance Corporation
AFZ	Air Force of Zimbabwe
ALOZ	Adult Literacy Association of Zimbabwe
AMA	Agricultural Marketing Authority
ARDA	Agricultural and Rural Development Authority
ARLAC	African Regional Labour Administration Centre
AWC	Association of Women's Clubs
CAB	Citizens Advice Bureau
CAPCO	Central Africa Power Corporation
CFU	Commercial Farmers' Union
CIO	Central Intelligence Organization
CMB	Cotton Marketing Board
CSC	Cold Storage Commission
CSO	Central Statistical Office
CZI	Confederation of Zimbabwe Industries
DDF	District Development Fund
DMB	Dairy Marketing Board
EMCOZ	Employers' Confederation of Zimbabwe
FVA	Film and Video Association
GMB	Grain Marketing Board
MMCZ	Minerals Marketing Corporation of Zimbabwe
NEDCO	Neighbourhood Development Committee

NOCZIM	National Oil Corporation of Zimbabwe
NRB	Natural Resources Board
NRZ	National Railways of Zimbabwe
(PF) ZAPU	(Patriotic Front) Zimbabwe African People's Union
ORAP	Organization of Rural Associations of Progress
POSB	Post Office Savings Bank
PTA	Preferential Trade Area
PTA	Parent Teacher Association
SADCC	Southern African Development Co-ordination Conference
SPCA	Society for the Prevention of Cruelty to Animals
UNICEF	United Nations Children's Fund
UNDP	United Nations Development Programme
UNHCR	United Nations High Commission for Refugees
VIDCO	Village Development Committee
WADCO	Ward Development Committee
WAG	Women's Action Group
YWCA	Young Women's Christian Association
ZANU (PF)	Zimbabwe African National Union (Patriotic Front)
ZAVACAD	Zimbabwe Association of Visual Artists, Craftsmen and Designers
ZBC	Zimbabwe Broadcasting Corporation
ZBC-TV	Zimbabwe Broadcasting Corporation–Television
ZBPA	Zimbabwe Book Publishers' Association
ZCTU	Zimbabwe Congress of Trade Unions
ZESA	Zimbabwe Electricity Supply Authority
ZIANA	Zimbabwe Inter-Africa News Agency
ZIMFEP	Zimbabwe Foundation for Education with Production
ZISCO	Zimbabwe Iron and Steel Company
ZMDC	Zimbabwe Mining Development Corporation
ZMMT	Zimbabwe Mass Media Trust
ZNA	Zimbabwe National Army
ZPM	Zimbabwe People's Militia
ZRP	Zimbabwe Republic Police

Zimbabwean Honours and Awards

Order of Merit
   Grand Master of the Legion of Merit (held only by the President)
   Grand Commander of the Zimbabwe Order of Merit (GCZM)
   Grand Officer of the Zimbabwe Order of Merit (GZM)
   Commander of the Zimbabwe Order of Merit (CZM)
   Officer of the Zimbabwe Order of Merit (OZM)
   Member of the Zimbabwe Order of Merit (MZM)
   Medal for Meritorious Service (MMS)

Bravery and Service Awards
   Gold Cross of Zimbabwe (GCZ)
   Silver Cross of Zimbabwe (SCZ)

	resistance is characterized by informal, isolated local resistance: independent churches, migration, evasion of tax, desertion, machine-breaking (on mines) crop burning (on white farms), spontaneous strikes, etc.
1914 –18	First World War; Rhodesian black and white troops involved.
1920s	Many Africans working and living in towns. Begin to see themselves as members of new classes. Begin to form new types of resistance organization.
1922	Rhodesian whites decide in referendum not to join Union of South Africa. End of BSAC rule 1923. Settlers given much local autonomy under system of 'Responsible Government'. Sir Charles Coghlan becomes first Prime Minister.
1927	Formation of Rhodesian Industrial and Commercial Union (RICU), the first black trade union.
1930	Land Apportionment Act passed, giving most productive land to whites and restricting African farmers to crowded and depleted reserves. Many more Africans forced to seek work on mines, farms and in towns.
1933	Sir Godfrey Huggins (later Lord Malvern) becomes Prime Minister; retains post until 1953.
1930s & 1940s	Growth of secondary industry and towns. More and more Africans move to live permanently in the towns.
1934	Formation of Southern Rhodesian African National Congress (SRANC, commonly referred to as ANC); mainly middle-class leadership but looks to workers for support.
1944	Formation of Rhodesia Railways African Employees Association (RRAEA), one of the first African industrial trade unions.
1945	National strike by black railway workers. First nationwide strike.
1946	Formation of Reformed Industrial and Commercial Workers Union (RICU) led by Charles Mzingeli; formation of British African National Voice Association (BANVA) led by Benjamin Burombo. Increasingly effective union organization. Number of strikes increases.
1948	African trade unions organize first General Strike.
1950s & 1960s	Number of strikes decreases as many trade unionists join the nationalist movement. Worker organization neglected as struggle shifts to rural guerilla warfare.
1951	Native Land Husbandry Act passed, by which land available to African farmers reduced. Overcrowding in reserves throws many more Africans on to the labour market.
1953	Establishment of Federation of Rhodesia and Nyasaland (also called Central African Federation).

1953–58	Southern Rhodesian Government led by Sir Garfield Todd. SR settlers benefit from wealth produced in Northern Rhodesia (Zambia) and Nyasaland (Malawi).
1954	Formation of Southern Rhodesian African Trades Union Congress led by Joshua Nkomo.
1955	Foundation of African National Youth League (ANYL); among founders were James Chikerema, George Nyandoro, Maurice Nyagumbo and Enoch Dumbutshena.
1956	Sir Roy Welensky becomes Prime Minister of Federation.
1957	ANYL & SRANC combine to form ANC with Nkomo as President and Chikerema as Vice-President.
1958	All African People's Conference in Ghana spurs leaders of Africa to free their countries from colonialism. Garfield Todd attempts to introduce reforms into Rhodesia. White settlers refuse to accept the reforms and elect Edgar Whitehead as PM.
1959	Dr Hastings Banda returns to Nyasaland; widespread anti-Federation agitation in federal territories; ANC banned in Southern Rhodesia and 500 people detained.
1960	Formation of National Democratic Party (NDP) led by Michael Mawema; members include Robert Mugabe, Moton Malianga, George Silundika, Eddison Zvobgo, Ndabaningi Sithole, Leopold Takawira, Herbert Chitepo and Enos Nkala; in July NDP leads march in Harare – 'March of the 7000' – protesting against the arrest of NDP leaders.
1961	Constitutional conference at Victoria Falls, resulting in the establishment of mainly separate white and black voters roles which entrenches white control of government; NDP (National Democratic Party) banned; formation in November of Zimbabwe African People's Union (ZAPU).
1962	Rhodesian Front (RF) party wins elections, white settlers prepare to go it alone; formation (in Tanzania) of the Front for the Liberation of Mozambique (FRELIMO) led by Eduardo Mondlane.
1963	Split in ZAPU leads to formation in August of Zimbabwe African National Union (ZANU) led by Ndabaningi Sithole; formation of the People's Caretaker Council (PCC) led by Nkomo; first recruits of ZANU's military wing, the Zimbabwe African National Liberation Army (ZANLA), go to China for training; Federation ends 31 December; formation of Organization of African Unity (OAU).
1964	Ian Smith becomes Prime Minister; ZANU and PCC banned and leaders detained.
1964	Zambia (Northern Rhodesia) and Malawi (Nyasaland) achieve their independence.

1965	RF re-elected in May; announce Unilateral Declaration of Independence in November.
1966	On 29 April first attack by ZANLA freedom fighters near Chinhoyi; (this date now celebrated as Chimurenga Day, marking the start of the War of Liberation); on *HMS Tiger* Rhodesian government refuses to accept British conditions for independence.
1966	Botswana (Bechuanaland) and Lesotho (Basutoland) become independent.
1967–68	Hwange campaign: extensive joint military operation of ZAPU & ANC (SA) in south-west Zimbabwe.
1968	Swaziland gains independence.
1968	Smith and British PM Wilson meet again on *HMS Fearless*; Smith still refuses to accept majority rule; United Nations imposes mandatory sanctions on Rhodesia.
1969	ZANLA forms 'Dare re Chimurenga' (war council); Rhodesian government passes Land Tenure Act upon which it builds policy of segregation.
1970	FRELIMO invites ZANLA to use Mozambique bases in liberated areas. Rhodesia declares itself a Republic.
1972	Pearce Commission arrives in January to test African response to new constitutional proposals; formation of African National Council (organized by ZANU & ZAPU leaders not in exile or prison and led by Abel Muzorewa); ZANU & ZAPU use this opportunity to organize people. The message for Pearce is an emphatic No! Start of ZANLA's north-east offensive.
1973	Rhodesia closes its border with Zambia (it remains closed until 1978).
1974	Portuguese government overthrown in revolution led by young army officers. FRELIMO takes over government in Mozambique; Rhodesian government forms the Mozambique National Resistance (MNR) to destabilize Mozambique and prevent FRELIMO giving support to ZANLA.
1975	Herbert Chitepo assassinated in Lusaka.
1975–80	ZIPRA intensifies war from Zambia. ZANLA & ZIPRA form ZIPA (Zimbabwe People's Army)
1976	Formation of Patriotic Front (PF). Guerrillas infiltrate along entire Eastern border. War escalates.
1976	Mozambique closes border with Rhodesia; USA and South Africa pressurize Smith to accept the principle of majority rule. First constitutional conference in Geneva; Rhodesian forces attack camps in Mozambique and Zambia killing thousands of Zimbabwean refugees.
1977	Assassination of J Z Moyo. Rhodesian forces attack Chimoio camp in Mozambique and kill over 1000 Zimbabweans; Robert Mugabe replaces Sithole as elected President of ZANU.

1979	Rhodesian non-racial elections in April, with Muzorewa becoming first Prime Minister. ZANLA & ZIPRA operate throughout Zimbabwe. Rhodesians only secure in major cities and towns.
1979	Formation of Zimbabwe-Rhodesia fails to end war; Smith eventually agrees to Lancaster House talks in London from September to December with British Government and the Patriotic Front (ZANU & ZAPU). Peace agreement signed 21 December; British Governor, Lord Soames, restored to supervise the independence process. ZIPRA & ZANLA freedom fighters regroup in assembly points.
1980	Elections in February won by ZANU (PF); on 18 April the Republic of Zimbabwe born, with R G Mugabe as Prime Minister and Canaan Banana as President; Zimbabwe joins SADCC; First Five-Year Development Plan introduced; integration of armed forces gets under way; first burials of national heroes' Acre (Jason Moyo and Josiah Tongogara).
1982	Arrest of leading (PF) ZAPU personnel and removal of (PF) ZAPU members of Cabinet following discovery of arms caches in Matabeleland.
1985	ZANU (PF) wins elections.
1986	Beira Corridor Project begins; Zimbabwe hosts eighth summit of Non-Aligned Movement (NAM) and Mugabe elected Chairman of NAM; death of Samora Machel.
1987	South African destabilization increases, with bombs planted in Harare and Bulawayo; on-going unity talks between ZANU (PF) and (PF) ZAPU; amendments to Lancaster House constitution, removing white seats; Mugabe sworn in as Executive President of Zimbabwe on 31 December.
1988	South African destabilization continues; merging of ZANU (PF) and (PF) ZAPU; appointment of Nkomo as a Vice-President of the Party.
1989	Unity complete.

CULTURAL INSTITUTIONS

National Art Gallery of Zimbabwe
20 Julius Nyerere Way/Park Lane, PO Box 8155, Causeway, Harare.

National Gallery, Bulawayo
Corner Selbourne Avenue and Grey Street, PO Box 1993, Bulawayo. The galleries promote the work of Zimbabwean visual artists by exhibiting their sculpture, paintings, drawings, pottery, etc., locally and overseas.

Gallery Shona Sculpture (Part of Chapungu Village)
Doon Estate, 1 Harrow Road, Beverley East, Massa, PO Box 2863, Harare.

They have a large collection of Shona sculpture and support artists by exhibiting their work locally and overseas.

Matombo Gallery
6 Zimre Centre, 114 Moffat Street, PO Box 5068, Harare.
Promotes visual arts in Zimbabwe by exhibiting locally and overseas.

Tengenenge Sculpture
38 Maidenhead Lane, Borrowdale, Harare.
Promotes visual arts in Zimbabwe by exhibiting the work of artists locally and overseas.

Gallery Delta
76 Manica Road, between 1st and Angwa Streets, PO Box UA 373, Union Avenue, Harare.
Specializes in fine arts.

Vukutu Gallery
Corner Blakiston/Harvey Brown Streets, Milton Park, PO Box 2072, Harare.
Specializes in local stone sculpture.

National Arts Council of Zimbabwe
144 Sinoia Street, PO Box UA 473, Union Avenue, Harare.
The Council promotes and administers all arts in Zimbabwe. It has nine Provincial Arts Councils and 55 District Arts Councils.

The National Museums and Monuments Headquarters
107 Rotten Row, PO Box 8540, Causeway, Harare.

There are museums in Harare, Bulawayo, Mutare, Gweru and Masvingo categorized as follows:

1. Harare – Ethnographic museum.
2. Bulawayo – Natural Sciences museum.
3. Mutare – Transport museum.
4. Gweru – Military museum.
5. Masvingo – National monument at Great Zimbabwe and a site museum.

The National Theatre Organization
Harvest House, Baker Avenue, PO Box 2701, Harare.
The function of this organization is to promote theatre arts in Zimbabwe.

The National Ballet
PO Box A423, Avondale, Harare.
This organization specializes in ballet dancing and training.

The National Dance Company
Presently with Ministry of Youth Sport and Culture, Makombe Complex Block 1, Corner Harare Street and Rhodes Avenue, Private Bag 7749, Causeway, Harare.
The Company specializes in traditional dance.

The National Archives

Borrowdale Road, Gunhill, Private Bag 7729, Causeway, Harare.
All important documents that are no longer in daily use are deposited
with the archives for reference.

The National Library and Documentation Service (NLDS),

Presently under Ministry of Youth Sport and Culture, Makombe
Building Complex Block 1, Corner Harare Street and Rhodes Avenue,
Private Bag 7749, Causeway, Harare.
This is the library and documentation service whose headquarters
will be situated in Harare. The NLDS offers library services to the
public and promotes works of literary arts.

Zimbabwe Literature Bureau

Electra House, Samora Machel Avenue, PO Box 8137, Causeway,
Harare.
The Literature Bureau specializes in the promotion of literary arts
such as poetry, novels, etc., particularly in indigenous languages.

The Crafts Council of Zimbabwe

PO Box 6674, Harare.
The Council deals with the promotion, development and marketing of
crafts.

ARTS AND CRAFTS CENTRES

Mzilikazi Art and Craft Centre

Taylor Avenue, Mzilikazi, Bulawayo.
The Centre specializes in the promotion of art and crafts.

Art is also taught at the BAT Workshop School, PO Box 8155, Causeway, Harare; the Harare Polytechnic, PO Box 8074, Causeway, Harare;
and Mount Hampden College, PO Box MR, 39 Marlborough, Harare.

COLLEGES OF MUSIC

Zimbabwe College of Music

Civic Centre, Rotten Row, Harare.

Zimbabwe Academy of Music

Hillside Road, Showgrounds, PO Box 1678, Bulawayo.

Midlands Academy of Music

Livingstone Avenue, P O Box 433, Gweru.
The colleges of music teach both classical and modern music.

EDUCATION

The Ministry of Primary and Secondary Education is based in Harare
and is responsible for all schools, colleges and the university.
Since Zimbabwe's Independence in 1980, there has been great expansion
in education, as the following figures show:

Number of	1979	1988
Primary schools	2401	4471
Secondary schools	177	1484
Total primary enrolment	819 586	2220967
Total secondary enrolment	66215	653343
Form IV	2141	112965

Primary Teachers' Training Colleges
1. Seke Teachers Training College, PO Box 11, Harare
2. Mkoba Teachers Training College, PO Box 20, Gweru
3. Mutare Teachers Training College, PO Box 3293, Paulington, Mutare
4. Nyadiri Teachers Training College, PO Box 210, Mutoko
5. United Teachers College, Private Bag T5392, Bulawayo
6. Bondolfi Teachers College, Private Bag 9050, Masvingo
7. Morgenster Teachers Training College, PO Morgenster, Masvingo

Zintec Colleges
1. Morgan Zintec, PO Box 1700, Harare
2. Gwanda Zintec, Private Bag 5852, Gwanda
3. Marymount Zintec, PO Box 20, Mutare
4. Andrew Louw Zintec, PO Box 790, Masvingo

Secondary Teachers Training Colleges
1. Belvedere Teachers Training College, PO Box BE 100, Belvedere, Harare
2. Gweru Teacher's Training College, Private Bag 9055, Gweru
3. Hillside teachers College, Private Bag 1, Hillside, Bulawayo
4. Masvingo Teachers Training College, PO Box 760, Masvingo.

University of Zimbabwe
PO Box MP 167, Mount Pleasant, Harare
There are 72 departments within ten faculties as follows:

Faculties:	Nos of students (1988)
Agriculture	370
Arts	1450
Commerce	1100
Education	960
Engineering	650
Law	320
Medicine	660
Science	970
Social Studies	1570
Veterinary Science	130

Technical Colleges
1. Bulawayo Technical College, PO Box 1392, Bulawayo.
2. Gweru Technical College, PO Box 137, Gweru.
3. Kwekwe technical College, PO Box 399, Kwekwe.

4. Kushinga Phikelela Technical College, PO Box 3716, Marondera.
5. Masvingo Technical College, PO Box 800, Masvingo.
6. Mutare Technical College, PO Box 640, Mutare.

The Ministry of Labour, Manpower Planning and Social Welfare in
Harare is responsible for vocational training throughout the country.
It should also be noted that most Ministries have an education and
training component. Details may be obtained by writing to them directly.

REGIONAL AND INTERNATIONAL GROUPINGS
Southern African Development Coordination Conference (SADCC)
This body, commonly known as SADCC, is an economic grouping of nine
southern African countries: Angola, Botswana, Lesotho, Malawi, Mozambique, Swaziland, Tanzania, Zambia and Zimbabwe.

The three southern African liberation movements, which have ob-
server status in SADCC, are the South West Africa People's Organization (SWAPO), the African National Congress (ANC) and the Pan-
Africanist Congress of Azania (PAC).

SADCC was formally launched in Lusaka, Zambia, on 1 April 1980. Its
headquarters are in Gaborone, the capital of Botswana.

Distribution of responsibilities:

Angola	Energy conservation and development
Botswana	Agricultural research and animal disease control
Lesotho	Soil and water conservation, land utilization and tourism
Malawi	Fisheries, wildlife and forestry
Mozambique	Transport and communications
Swaziland	Co-ordination of manpower training and develop-ment
Tanzania	Industrial development
Zambia	Mining
Zimbabwe	Regional food security

Preferential Trade Area (PTA)
This body, officially known as the Preferential Trade Area for Eastern
and Southern Africa but often referred to by the abbreviation PTA, was
set up in 1981. It is an economic union which aims to serve the interests
of the following countries:

Angola, Botswana, Comoros, Djibouti, Ethiopia, Kenya, Lesotho,
Madagascar, Malawi, Mozambique, Seychelles, Somalia, Swaziland,
Tanzania, Uganda, Zambia, Zimbabwe.

Organization of African Unity (OAU)
All the countries of Africa, apart from Namibia, South Africa and the
Saharawi Republic, are members of this organization. It is usually
referred to as the OAU.

The headquarters of the OAU are in Addis Ababa, the capital of

POLITICAL, ECONOMIC AND CONTINENTAL GROUPINGS

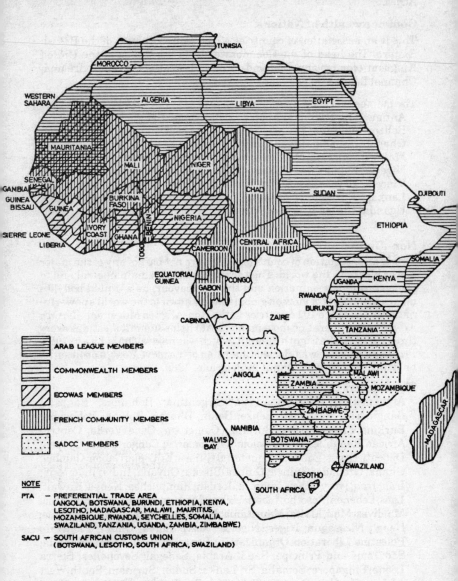

ARAB LEAGUE MEMBERS

COMMONWEALTH MEMBERS

ECOWAS MEMBERS

FRENCH COMMUNITY MEMBERS

SADCC MEMBERS

NOTE

PTA — PREFERENTIAL TRADE AREA
(ANGOLA, BOTSWANA, BURUNDI, ETHIOPIA, KENYA,
LESOTHO, MADAGASCAR, MALAWI, MAURITIUS,
MOZAMBIQUE, RWANDA, SEYCHELLES, SOMALIA,
SWAZILAND, TANZANIA, UGANDA, ZAMBIA, ZIMBABWE)

SACU — SOUTH AFRICAN CUSTOMS UNION
(BOTSWANA, LESOTHO, SOUTH AFRICA, SWAZILAND)

Ethiopia. The OAU is a political union and supports several liberation movements in Africa, particularly those seeking democracy in South Africa.

Commonwealth of Nations

This is an association of countries which were once part of the British Empire. The head of the Commonwealth is the Queen of the United Kingdom (comprising England, Scotland, Wales, Northern Ireland, Channel Islands, Isle of Man).

The members of the Commonwealth are:

Antigua and Barbuda; Australia; Bahamas; Bangladesh; Barbados; Belize; Botswana; Brunei; Canada; Cyprus; Dominica; Fiji; Gambia; Ghana; Grenada; Guyana; India; Jamaica; Kenya; Kiribati; Lesotho; Malawi; Malaysia; Maldives; Malta; Mauritius; Nauru; New Zealand; Nigeria; Papua New Guinea; St Christopher and Nevis; St Lucia; St Vincent; Seychelles; Sierra Leone; Singapore; Solomon Islands; Sri Lanka; Swaziland; Tanzania; Tonga; Trinidad and Tobago; Tuvalu; Uganda; United Kingdom; Vanuatu; Western Samoa; Zambia; Zimbabwe.

Non-Aligned Movement (NAM)

This is an association of countries which are not part of any of the major power blocks in the world. They share a wish to remain neutral and to promote self-determination and they endeavour, as a united body, to make their points of view on global issues known to the world's powerful nations. There are 101 countries in the Non-Aligned Movement (NAM), as well as two liberation movements. NAM holds summit meetings every three years. At the Eighth Summit, which was held in Zimbabwe in 1986, President Mugabe was elected Chairman of the movement, a position he held until the Ninth Summit in Belgrade, 1989.

The members of NAM are:

Afghanistan; Algeria; Angola; Argentina; Bahamas; Bahrain; Bangladesh; Barbados; Belize; Benin; Bhutan; Bolivia; Botswana; Burkina Faso; Burma; Burundi; Cameroon; Cape Verde; Central African Republic; Chad; Colombia; Comores; Congo; Cuba; Cyprus; Djibouti; Egypt; Equador; Equatorial Guinea; Ethiopia; Gabon; Gambia; Ghana; Grenada; Guinea; Guinea-Bissau; Guyana; India; Indonesia; Iran; Iraq; Ivory Coast; Jamaica; Jordan; Kampuchea; Kenya; Kuwait; Laos; Lebanon; Lesotho; Liberia; Libya; Madagascar; Malawi; Malaysia; Maldives; Mali; Malta; Mauritania; Mauritius; Morocco; Mozambique; Nepal; Nicaragua; Niger; Nigeria; North Korea; Oman; Pakistan; Palestine Liberation Organization; Panama; Peru; Qatar; Ruanda; São Tomé and Principe; Saudi Arabia; Senegal; Seychelles; Sierra Leone; Singapore; Somalia; Sri Lanka; Sudan; Surinam; South West African People's Organization; Swaziland; Syria; Tanzania; Togo; Trinidad and Tobago; Tunisia; Uganda; United Arab Emirates; Vanuatu; Vietnam; Yemen (Aden); Yemen (Sana); Yugoslavia; Zambia; Zaïre; Zimbabwe.

PART TWO

Famous People

This section introduces some famous names from (a) southern Africa, and (b) the rest of the world. The list cannot begin to be exhaustive, nor are the biographies more than brief introductions. If you want additional information, you are urged to consult reference sources in your library.

SOUTHERN AFRICA

Abrahams, Peter
(1919–) South African writer, whose powerful writing had considerable influence on later black writers. Born in Johannesburg, he went to England in 1941, then settled in Jamaica. Graduated from protest-poet to novelist with the publication of *Song of the City* (1945), *Mine Boy* (1946) and *The Path of Thunder* (1948). In *A Wreath for Udomo* (1956), he wrote of black independence. Autobiography: *Tell Freedom* (1945).

Baines, Thomas
(1820–1875) English artist who accompanied David Livingstone on travels through southern Africa in the 1860s. He produced paintings of life in Zimbabwe at that time, particularly of the Victoria Falls and the Zambezi River region. Many of these paintings have become world-famous.

Banana, Canaan
(1936–) Theologian and politician who was a founder member of African National Council in 1971 and joined the Zimbabwe African National Union in 1976, becoming its publicity secretary. He spent much time in detention in the 1960s and 1970s. In 1980, he was appointed first President of Zimbabwe and held this position until 1987.

Biko, Stephen Bantu
(1946–1977) South African activist and Black Consciousness leader. First president of SA Student Organization, 1968; expelled from medical studies at Natal University in 1969; founded Black People's Convention, 1969. Banned in 1973 and restricted to Kingwilliam's Town for five years. First detained without trial for 137 days in 1975; remained active as acknowledged leader while under restriction. Detained in August 1977 in Port Elizabeth, he was driven naked to Pretoria, where he died from results of police interrogation.

Blair, Dyson
(1907–1978) Scientist who devoted much research to the promotion of health in rural areas in the 1950s and 1960s and became a consultant to the World Health Organization. The Blair Research Laboratory in Harare is named after him, as is the Blair latrine, a major development technology success widely used in Zimbabwe and spreading to much of Africa.

23

Botha, Pieter Willem – 'PW'

(1916–) South African politician, State President till 1989. Interrupted his law studies to become National Party organizer in 1936 and remained a party functionary all his life. Succeeded Vorster as Prime Minister in 1978, introduced a new constitution in 1984, with himself as Executive President. He reluctantly retired in 1989 after party elected F.W de Klerk as new leader and President.

Brink, Andre

(1935–) South African Afrikaans novelist whose works expose the ambiguity and evils of apartheid. *Looking on Darkness* (1973) was the first Afrikaans novel to be banned in South Africa. Professor of Afrikaans and Dutch literature at Rhodes University since 1961, his other novels include: *An Instant in the Wind* (1976), *Rumours of Rain* (1978), *A Chain of Voices* (1981), *The Wall of The Plaque* (1984), *A Dry White Season* (1979) and *States of Emergency* (1989).

Burombo, Benjamin

(c.1909–1958) Trade unionist who founded the British African National Voice Association in 1947. This was the beginning of mass nationalism in Zimbabwe, and BANVA's success in voicing workers' discontent led to the 1948 general strike. Burombo also campaigned on behalf of the peasants against the Land Apportionment Act of 1930. In 1957 he travelled throughout the country laying the foundations for a mass political party.

Caton-Thompson, Gertrude

(1888–1985) English archaeologist who in 1928–29 investigated the origins of Great Zimbabwe and other stone building sites in Zimbabwe. She concluded that they were not built by foreigners, such as Arabs and Phoenicians, but by Bantu-speaking Africans. The results of her work, published in 1931, remain the cornerstone of archaeological work in Zimbabwe.

Chikerema, James Robert Dambaza

(1925–) One of Zimbabwe's first nationalist leaders. Became a member of the ANC in South Africa in 1944 as a student. Entered politics in Rhodesia in 1955; imprisoned from 1959–63, he went into exile in Zambia on his release. Left ZAPU to help found FROLIZI, of which he became President. Tried to unite all the nationalist parties under the ANC, but when ZANU and ZAPU broke away from the other nationalist movements, Chikerema joined the ANC. Minister with the government of Zimbabwe-Rhodesia, he left the UANC to form his own party, the Zimbabwe Democratic Party, which was dissolved after losing 1980 elections. Resigned from politics and went into private business.

Chinamano, Josiah

1922–1984) Zimbabwean teacher and politician, born at Epworth Mission. Educated at Waddilove, where he taught before graduating from Fort Hare. Returned home as a headmaster, taught in England for a year in 1955, then returned and became founder headmaster of Highfield

Community School. On first Executive Committee of ZAPU in 1961; detained for five years from 1964. In 1971 became treasurer of newly-formed ANC; arrested and spent two-and-a-half years in prison. Appointed to Central Committee of ANC and later ZAPU, he attended Victoria Falls and Geneva talks. At Independence, appointed Minister of Transport, but lost Cabinet post in 1982. Buried at Heroes' Acre.

Chissano, Joaquim

(1939–) President of Mozambique who, after studying in Portugal, joined the Front for the Liberation of Mozambique (FRELIMO) in 1963. At independence in 1975 he became Mozambique's Minister of Foreign Affairs and in 1986, after the death of Samora Machel, he assumed the Presidency at a time when the activities of South African-backed bandits were causing the displacement and death of thousands of Mozambicans.

Chitepo, Herbert Wiltshire Hamandini

(1923–1975) National Chairman of ZANU and Zimbabwe's first black advocate, he successfully defended many early Zimbabwean nationalists. This legal achievement led to him becoming the Director of Public Prosecution in Tanzania. Following the ban on ZANU, he went to Zambia to lead the Revolutionary Council where he restructured the Party to make it more efficient. He was killed by a car-bomb in Lusaka. His remains were reburied at Heroes' Acre in 1981.

Danbarembga, Tsitsi

(1954–) Zimbabwean writer, who has studied medicine and psychology. She has published a volume of plays, *She No Longer Weeps* (1988); her novel, *Nervous Conditions*, won the Commonwealth Writer's Prize for Africa in 1989. Now studying film-making.

Dumbutshena, Enoch

(1920–) Chief Justice of Zimbabwe. Joined the ANC in 1947 but resigned as Vice-President of the party in 1948 while remaining supportive of the nationalist cause. Studied law in London and worked briefly as an advocate in Rhodesia during the early 1960s, the third black to do so after Herbert Chitepo and Edson Sithole. In 1967, he was denied travel documents so crossed illegally into Zambia to practise, again providing support for nationalist cause. Returned to Zimbabwe at Independence and became Chief Justice in 1983.

Fugard, Athol

(1932–) South African playwright and pioneer of multi-racial theatre, whose plays deal with the human realities and miseries caused by apartheid. Achieved international recognition with *The Blood Knot* (1963). Other works include *Hello and Goodbye* (1966), *Boesman and Lena* (1969), *Siswe Banzi is Dead* (1974) and *The Island* (1974).

Gibbs, Sir Humphrey

(1902–) Governor of Rhodesia at the time of the Unilateral Declaration of Independence in 1965. He arrived in this country in 1928 and established a farm near Bulawayo. He was appointed Governor in 1959 but because of his opposition to UDI became a virtual prisoner in

Government House, Harare, where he lived until he resigned in 1969, the year in which he was knighted.

Gordimer, Nadine

(1923–) South African writer and critic, whose work examines the dilemmas, amorality, inertia and possibilities for opposition, reflected in the different positions adopted by whites living within the apartheid society. As a critic and member of a privileged minority, she has ruthlessly examined the role of the (white) writers within a repressive regime. Her novels include: *A World of Strangers* (1958), *Occasion for Loving* (1963), *The Late Bourgeois World* (1966), *A Guest of Honour* (1970), *The Conservationist* (1974), *Burger's Daughter* (1979), *July's People* (1981), *A Sport of Nature* (1987).

Haimutyinei, Mordekai

(1934–) Zimbabwean author and poet who has worked both as teacher and editor. Works include poetry: *Mabvumira Enhetembo* and *Nhetembo*: novels: *Maidei, Kusasana Kunoparira, Chinamanenji Hachifambisi* and *Ndi Kandei Mugebena*: and three plays, *Sungai Mbabvu*.

Head, Bessie

(1937–1986) South African writer who lived in exile in Botswana and whose work explores the inner personal experience. *When Rain Clouds Gather* (1969) describes her flight from South Africa to Botswana. *Maru* (1971) is a careful study of the ways of Botswana people. *A Question of Power* (1973) is a complex novel of exile and adjustment.

Hove, Chenjerai

(1954–) Zimbabwean journalist, novelist and poet, who has written in both Shona and English. Published anthologies of poetry include *Up in Arms* and *Red Hills of Home*. His first novel in English, *Bones*, won the 1989 Noma Award for publishing in Africa.

Jiri, Jairos

(1921–1982) Bulawayo philanthropist who in the 1940s began devoting himself to the care of disabled. He founded an association to provide rehabilitation facilities for the disabled people throughout Zimbabwe. The Jairos Jiri Association is now one of Zimbabwe's leading charity institutions.

Kaguvi, Gomboreshumba

(1860s?–1898) Spirit medium who played an influential role during Zimbabwe's First Chimurenga. He surrendered in 1897, was found guilty of murder and on 17 April 1898 was executed. He was popularly known as 'Murenga' (meaning 'resister'), from which the word 'Chimurenga' was derived to describe liberation struggles in Zimbabwe.

Kaunda, Kenneth

(1924–) President of Zambia since 1964. He joined the African National Congress in the 1950s and was its Secretary-General from 1953 to 1958. He formed the Zambian African National Congress and later became President of the United National Independence Party. He was Chairman of the Non-Aligned Movement from 1970 to 1973, and is current Chairman of the Frontline States. He has written a number of books, including *A Humanist in Africa*.

La Guma, Alex

(1925–1985) South African writer, born in Cape Town. A political activist, he was banned and frequently detained. He went into exile in London in 1966, where he stayed until becoming the ANC's representative in Cuba in 1978. His first and best-known novel, *A Walk in the Night* (1962), is set in Cape Town's 'Coloured' area, District Six. *Time of the Butcherbird* (1979) explores the re-settlement of urban people.

Lessing, Doris

(1919–) Author who has gained world-wide recognition for her novels, many of which are based on her early life in Zimbabwe. She joined the trade union movement in 1940 and her pro-nationalist and anti-settler sympathies were the themes of her well-known books *The Grass is Singing*, the *Children of Violence* novels and *The Golden Notebook*.

Livingstone, David

(1913–1873) Scottish missionary and explorer of Africa who opened much of central Africa up to missionary endeavours and thus to European settlement. He was the first white man to see the Victoria Falls, which he named after the then British Queen. He died while searching for the source of the River Nile.

Lobengula

(c.1836–1894) Ndebele king who succeeded his father, Mzilikazi, in 1870. He consolidated the Ndebele state and maintained strict control over white explorers, traders and missionaries entering his territory. He was tricked into signing the Rudd Concession, giving Cecil Rhodes the opening to set up the British South Africa Company and invade Mashonaland in 1890. The Company forces invaded the Ndebele state in 1893 and Lobengula fled northwards. He reportedly died of smallpox near Kamativi.

Luthuli, Chief Albert Myumbi

(1998–1967) South African politician known as the father of Black Nationalism. Born in Zimbabwe, his family returned to South Africa in 1908. Joined the African National Congress in 1945. Told to choose between his chieftainship and his membership of the ANC, he chose the latter and lost the former. In 1951 he was made President-General of the ANC, a post he held until his death. Frequently banned, imprisoned, and put under house arrest, he was awarded the Nobel Peace Prize in 1960. His autobiography *Let My People Go* was published in 1961.

Macgregor, Alexander

(1888–1961) Scientist who is regarded as the Father of Geology in Zimbabwe. He became Director of the Department of Geological Survey and wrote many papers which attracted international attention. In 1947 he produced the first overall account of the geology of Zimbabwe.

Machel, Samora

(1933–1986) Late President of Mozambique who became a great African statesman. After training as a medical assistant he joined the Front for the Liberation of Mozambique (FRELIMO) in 1963 and became its President in 1969 after the assassination of Edouardo Mondlane. When Mozambique achieved independence in 1975 Machel became President. He died in a mysterious aeroplane crash over South Africa.

Makhalisa, Barbara

(1949–) Zimbabwean author and editor, who began her career as a teacher. Her works include *Impilo Vinkinga* (novel, 1974) and *The Underdog and other stories* (1974), *Qilindini* (novel, 1975), *Umendo* (novel, 1977), *Umhlaba ho!* (play, 1977).

Mapanje, Jack

(1947–) Malawi's best-known poet, critic and writer. Author of *Of Chameleons and Gods*. Head of the English department at the University of Malawi, and the Southern African Linguistics Association, he was detained by his government in 1987.

Mapfumo, Thomas

(1945–) Zimbabwean musician. One of the first to use music as a vehicle for political messages. Formed his own group, the Blacks Unlimited, in 1975. During the liberation struggle, Mapfumo included revolutionary messages in his songs, which were banned on air, but he continued to popularize them at live shows. Detained for 90 days without trial in 1979. Has won many awards for his music, widely known as Chimurenga music.

Mandela, Nelson

(1918–) South African political leader who has become a symbol of hope and resistance for the people of South Africa seeking to dismantle apartheid. He trained as a lawyer and co-founded the African National Congress Youth League. From 1956 to 1961 he was on trial for treason; after acquittal, he went underground and was re-arrested in 1962. In 1964 he was sentenced to life imprisonment at the Rivonia Trial. He was held on Robben Island, before being moved in 1988 to a prison reserve in Cape Town. Among his books is *No Easy Walk to Freedom*.

Marechera, Dambudzo

(1952–1987) Zimbabwean author whose writing won him international acclaim. Among his most important works are *The House of Hunger*, which was published in 1978 and won the 1980 Guardian Fiction Prize, *Black Sunlight* (1980) and *Mindblast* (1984).

Matamera, Bernard

(1946–) Zimbabwean sculptor. One of the earliest members of the Tengenenge sculpture community, which he joined after having shown talent at wood-carving while at school. His work has been exhibited in India, Australia and West Germany. In 1986 he won first prize in the National Gallery of Zimbabwe's annual exhibition.

Masire, Quett

(1925–) President of Botswana who succeeded the late Sir Seretse Khama. He was a founder member of the Botswana Democratic Party and became its Secretary-General. In 1967 he was appointed Minister of Development Planning and thereafter was regarded as the obvious successor to Sir Seretse.

Mkwati

(? – 1897) Ndebele who played a significant role during the First Chimurenga by relaying to the Shona people news of the uprising in Matabeleland. After Kaguvi's arrest in 1897 he fled northwards but was killed by local people. His belief in the need for Shona and Ndebele unity to resist the white settlers was an inspiration in the Second Chimurenga.

Moyo, Jason Ziyaphapha

(1927–1977) Zimbabwean carpenter, builder and trade unionist, member and then Chairman of the ANC in the 1950s. His political activities led to his detention in 1959. Subsequently held executive positions in the NDP, ZAPU and PCC but when each of these parties was banned, he went to Lusaka as a member of ZAPU's external wing. Worked closely with ZIPRA and in 1976 was made second vice-president of ZAPU. Killed by a parcel bomb in Zambia. His remains were interred at Heroes' Acre in 1980.

Mphahlele, Es'kia

(1919–) South African teacher and writer. Banned for his opposition to the Bantu Education Act, he left South Africa in 1957 and travelled in Africa and America but, unable to write creatively away from his roots, he returned in 1978 and is now Professor of African Literature at the University of the Witwatersrand. His early works were angry protest stories such as *Man Must Live* (1974), *The Living and The Dead* (1961). *Down Second Avenue* (1959) is his life story up until he left South Africa. His first novel, *The Wanderers* (1971), examines the plight of an exile.

Mugabe, Robert Gabriel

(1924–) Politician who is regarded as one of Africa's most outstanding statesmen. He trained as a teacher and was elected Publicity Secretary of the National Democratic Party in 1960; he held the same position for the Zimbabwe African People's Union in 1961. He was instrumental in the formation of the Zimbabwe African National Union in 1963 and became ZANU's General Secretary. In 1964 he was arrested and imprisoned for ten years. After his release he escaped to Mozambique and in 1976 was elected President of ZANU. He was joint leader of the Patriotic Front at the Lancaster House talks in 1979 and led ZANU (PF) to victory in the 1980 elections, becoming the first Prime Minister of the Republic of Zimbabwe. In 1986 he was elected Chairman of the Non-Aligned Movement and, on 31 December 1987, became Executive President of Zimbabwe.

Mukarobgwa, Thomas

(1924–) Zimbabwean sculptor. Joined the National Gallery as an attendant in 1957, where he first began to paint and then to sculpt. Since 1966 his work, which is inspired by Shona traditional myths and beliefs, has been exhibited in Zimbabwe and Europe.

Mukomberanwa, Nicholas

(1940–) Zimbabwean sculptor. First began to carve at Serima Mission under Father Groeber. In 1961, he joined the police and became a part-time member of the Workshop school. He has worked full-time as a sculptor since 1976. Has exhibited in Europe, America and Australia.

Mungoshi, Charles

(1947–) One of Zimbabwe's foremost writers, whose writing has received international acclaim. His Shona novels include *Mukunun'unu Maodzo-mwayo, Ndiko Kupindana Kwamazuva* and *Kunyarara Hakusi Kutaura*; English works include *Coming of the Dry Season* (short stories), *Waiting for the Rain* and *Some Kinds of Wounds*. His poems have been published in *The Milkman Doesn't Only Deliver Milk*. Mungoshi has worked as an editor and is currently devoting all his time to writing.

Munyaradzi, Henry

(1931–) One of Zimbabwe's leading sculptors. Spent his early working life as village blacksmith, carpenter and a tobacco grader. In 1967 he joined the Tengenenge sculptor community and soon began to partici-pate in exhibitions. Today his work is internationally known; he has held one-man exhibitions in London and Los Angeles.

Muzenda, Simon

(1922–) Zimbabwe's Vice-President. Worked with Benjamin Burombo in the 1940s and was appointed Secretary-General of the British African National Voice Association in 1953. He joined the National Democratic Party in 1961 and spent much of the 1962–1971 period in prison. He helped build up the Zimbabwe African National Union in Zambia in the early 1970s and in 1980 became Deputy Prime Minister of Zimbabwe. In 1987 he became Vice-President of Zimbabwe.

Mzilikazi

(1792–1868) Ndebele king who broke away from the Zulu king, Shaka, and moved through the Transvaal and Botswana to western Zimbabwe, where he arrived in 1838. He established the Ndebele state in what is now Matabeleland and was succeeded by his son, Lobengula.

Mzingeli, Charles

(1905–1977) Zimbabwean trade unionist who founded the Industrial Commercial Workers Union in the 1920s and became a focal point of political activism in the 1930s and 1940s. He was interim Chairman of the All-Africa Convention set up to oppose the Federation of Rhodesia and Nyasaland. His trade union work is seen as a significant contribu-tion to the rise of mass nationalism.

Nehanda, Mbuya

(1862–1898) Spirit medium   prominent in north-eastern Zimbabwe during the First Chimurenga, urging Shona people to rise against the white settlers. Captured in 1897, she was found guilty of murder. At her execution on 17 April 1898 she sang that her death would not be in vain. Her heroism became an inspiration during the Second Chimurenga.

Neto, Agostinho

(1922–1979) Angolan politician and poet. Trained as a doctor and was imprisoned for a year in Lisbon. In 1962 he escaped from prison, returned to Africa and became President of the Movimento Popular de Libertacao de Angola, the party which formed the government of Angola at Independence in 1975, when he became first President of Angola.

Nkomo, Joshua

(1917–) Politician who became leader of the African National Congress in 1952 and President of the National Democratic Party in 1960. His subsequent political activities, including the founding of the Zimbabwe African People's Union and the People's Caretaker Council, led to a long detention. He led the ZAPU struggle for independence and became a member of the first Cabinet after the 1980 elections. In 1987, after successful unity talks between ZAPU and ZANU(PF), he became a Senior Minister in the Cabinet.

Nujoma, Sam

(1929–) President of the South West Africa People's Organization (SWAPO) since its birth in 1959. He initiated SWAPO's armed struggle against South Africa in 1966 and continued to lead the movement seeking Namibia's independence from South African control. Returned home after 30 years in exile in 1989.

Nyamfukudza, Stanley

(1951–) Zimbabwean writer. Expelled from the University of Rhodesia in 1973, he studied literature at Oxford. An editor in Harare until 1989, his works include *The Non-Believer's Journey* (1983) and two volumes of short stories, *Aftermaths* (1982) and *If God was a Woman* (1989).

Parirenyatwa, Dr Tichafa Samuel

(1922–1962) Zimbabwean politician and physician. When he qualified in 1957, he became Zimbabwe's first African doctor. He resigned from practice in 1961 to devote his time to politics. He was Vice-President of ZAPU at its formation in 1962. He was killed in a car accident.

Park, Merle

(1937–) Dancer who studied ballet in Zimbabwe as a child and was accepted by the Royal Ballet in Britain at the age of 15. She became the Royal Ballet's Principal Soloist in 1960, partnering such world-renowned dancers as Rudolf Nureyev. She was made a Dame of the British Empire in 1986.

Paton, Alan

(1903–1988) South African author who gained fame as an articulate and passionate opponent of apartheid after publication of his first novel, *Cry the Beloved Country*, in 1948. Co-founder of the South African Liberal Party. His second novel, *Too Late the Phalarope* (1955), was followed by many writings, including autobiography and short stories.

Patrick, Mother

(1863–1900) Roman Catholic Dominican nun who led a team of nursing sisters to Mashonaland in 1891. She set up a hospital and helped found the Dominican Convent in Harare. She was awarded the Royal Red Cross medal for her nursing work among people of all races and in 1899 became Prioress of the Dominican Order in Mashonaland.

Rhodes, Cecil John

(1853–1902) British-born financier and politician who wished to see the spread of British influence in Africa from the 'Cape to Cairo'. He amassed a fortune from diamond mining in South Africa and was elected to the Cape Parliament. In 1889 he formed the British South Africa Company whose forces occupied Mashonaland in 1890 and invaded Matabeleland in 1893. Rhodesia was named after him in 1895.

Samkange, Professor Stanlake James Thompson

(1922–1988) Teacher, historian, journalist, who founded Nyatsime College and the magazine, *The African Businessman*. He was also Secretary General of the Southern Rhodesian African National Congress in the late 'forties and Chairman of the Salisbury District branch of ZANU at its inception in 1963. He published a number of books including *On Trial for my Country* (1966) and *The Origins of Rhodesia* (1968).

Shaka

(c.1787–1828) Zulu chief. Soldier in Dingiswayo's army, he became renowned for his bravery. Made a chief after the death of his father, Shaka established his rule through the efficiency of his army, based on the use of the assegai and large, linking shields. Renowned for his strict leadership yet attention to the welfare of his troops, his series of wars (the Mfecane) established Zulu nation as the strongest in southern Africa. Stabbed to death by his half-brothers, Dingane and Mhlangana.

Sigogo, Ndabezinhle

(1932–) Zimbabwean writer who worked as a teacher before joining the Department of Internal Affairs. Left government in 1969 to become an editor, first with Mambo Press, then with the Literature Bureau. His novels include *Usethi Ebakhweni Bakhe* (1962), *Gudlindlu Mntanami* (1967), *Akalazulu Emhlabeni* (1971), *Indlalifa Ngubani* (1976), *Akugoho Lingeqondiswe* (1981), *Veyeni Madoda* (1982), *Asazi-ke* (1986), *Ngenziwa Ngumumo Welinzwe* (1986). He has published two volumes of poetry: *Ihundla Vezimbongi* (1979) and *Umdomo Wezinkondlo* (1983).

Sithole, Edson Furatidzayi Chisingaitwi

(1935–75) One of Zimbabwe's first nationalist leaders. He held positions in the City Youth League, the Zimbabwe National Party and the Pan-African Socialist Union in the '50s; in 1964 he became Publicity Secretary for ZANU. Arrested and spent seven years in prison, where he obtained a doctorate in law. Became Rhodesia's second black attorney. On release, became Publicity Secretary for the ANC but in 1974 was again imprisoned. In 1975 he was kidnapped in Harare – presumably by agents of the Rhodesian Special Branch–and not seen again.

Sithole, Rev. Ndabaningi

(1920–) Founder member of ZAPU. Following disagreements within the party, he formed ZANU in 1963 together with Robert Mugabe and Leopold Takawira and became President. In 1969 while in detention, he was tried for plotting to assassinate Ian Smith and imprisoned for six years. He was removed from the ZANU leadership in 1974 when he denounced the armed struggle. In 1978, with Bishop Muzorewa and Chief Chirau, he supported the transitional government. He then formed his own ZANU party, which lost heavily in the 1980 elections. In 1983, he went into self-imposed exile in America.

Silundika, Tarcissius George

(1929–81) First Minister of Roads, Road Traffic, Posts and Telecommunications in independent Zimbabwe. Active politically from his student days, in South Africa, he became an executive member of the ANC, NDP and ZAPU before they were banned. Sent to Lusaka in 1963 to direct the first stages of the armed struggle, he became a leading member of ZIPRA. He was ZAPU MP for Matabeleland South and a Minister at the time of his death. Buried at Heroes' Acre.

Smith, Ian Douglas

(1919–) Politician who in 1961 helped form the Dominion Party, which later became the Rhodesian Front. After the RF election victory in 1962 he became Deputy Prime Minister and in 1964 replaced the Prime Minister, Winston Field. He announced the Unilateral Declaration of Independence in 1965, launching the country into a 15-year civil war during which he strongly resisted the idea of majority rule. He was succeeded by Bishop Abel Muzorewa in 1979 and continued to lead the right-wing white party after Independence until his resignation in 1987.

Sobukwe, Robert Mangaliso

(1924–78) South African political leader, first President of the Pan-Africanist Congress (PAC). Born in Graaff-Reinet, first achieved prominence as a student at Fort Hare. Lecturer in African Languages at University of Witwatersrand. Leader of the PAC from its break-away from ANC in 1959. Imprisoned on Robben Island following anti-pass law demonstrations and the massacre at Sharpeville in 1960. Released in 1969 but confined to Kimberley where he died.

Stanley, Sir Henry

(1841–1904) British explorer and journalist, sent in 1869 to find David Livingstone who was 'lost' in Africa. His famous meeting with Livingstone was in 1871 at Ujiji in Tanzania. Stanley continued as an explorer, leading an expedition which traced the Nile's source, circumnavigated Lakes Victoria and Tanganyika and traced the course of the Congo River.

Takawira, Bernard

(1945–) Zimbabwean sculptor. Began his working life as an agricultural extension assistant but, encouraged by his brother, John, began to sculpt. Considered among the most spiritual and deep-thinking of Zimbabwe's contemporary sculptors, his work is recognized world-wide.

Takawira, John

(1938–1989) Zimbabwean sculptor. One of the first members of the National Gallery's Workshop school, he began carving in 1962. His work, which reflects Shona ancestral beliefs, is among the finest in Zimbabwe and is represented·in art galleries throughout the world.

Takawira, Leopold Tapfumaneyi

(1916–1970) First Vice-President of ZANU. Educated at Kutama Mission and Roma University in Lesotho. First became active in politics when he taught at Chipembere Primary School and became member of the NDP, soon after becoming leader of the party and, subsequently, their external representative in London. When the NDP was banned, Takawira became external secretary of ZAPU. After ZAPU was banned, he helped form ZANU and became the first Vice-President. Arrested in Harare, he spent the rest of his life in prison, where he died after not being treated for diabetes. Reburied at Heroes' Acre in 1982.

Tangwena, Chief Rekayi Magodo

(1910–1984) Chief of the Tangwena people of Nyanga, who strongly resisted the decision by the Smith Government to move them from their land. During the liberation war he helped Robert Mugabe and Edgar Tekere to cross the border into Mozambique. A fearless critic of oppression, Chief Tangwena became a Senator in 1980. Buried at Heroes' Acre.

Todd, Sir Garfield

(1908–) New Zealand-born politician and missionary who became Prime Minister of Southern Rhodesia in 1953. His support of the advancement of the African cause led to his resignation in 1958. He formed the multiracial Central African Party in 1959. His outspoken criticism of the Rhodesian Front government led to his restriction at his home at Dadaya Mission and to imprisonment. He was appointed to the Senate after Independence and knighted in 1986.

Tongogara, General Josiah Magama

(1940–1979) Commander of the ZANLA forces during Zimbabwe's liberation war. Member of the ZANU youth wing, he received his military training in China and subsequently trained ZANU cadres in Mozambique. In 1972 he was appointed Military Commander of ZANLA and Chairman of the High Command. In 1974 was made Chief of Defence in the ZANU Supreme Council. In 1977 he became Secretary for Defence on the ZANU Central Committee, where he played an important role at the Lancaster House Conference. 'Cde Tongo' died in a car accident in Mozambique. His remains were buried at Heroes' Acre in 1982.

Tutu, Desmond Mpilo

(1931–) Anglican Archbishop of Cape Town and Nobel Peace Prize-winner. Ordained priest in 1961, he became Dean of Johannesburg in 1975, then Bishop of Lesotho, (1976–1978) and Secretary-General of the South African Council of Churches (1978). Always an outspoken critic of apartheid, he was awarded the Nobel Peace Prize in 1984, he was elected Bishop of Johannesburg in 1985 and, as Archbishop of Cape Town, became the first black leader of South African Anglicans in 1986.

Vambe, Lawrence

(1917–) One of the first Zimbabwean writers to achieve international recognition, with *The Ill-fated People* (1972) and *From Rhodesia to Zimbabwe* (1976). Began his working life as a teacher, then joined African Newspapers in 1946 as proof-reader. By the time he left in 1959 to join the diplomatic service, he was Editor-in-Chief. Information attaché in London till 1962, he began his business career in London in 1970 and returned to Zimbabwe at Independence. Chairman of the British-Zimbabwe Society.

Zvobgo, Dr Eddison Jonas Mudadirwa

(1935–) Zimbabwean Minister of State for Political Affairs. Born in Masvingo province. Graduate of the University of Lesotho. Founder member of the NDP in 1960. Detained in 1971, he graduated in Law whilst in prison. He spoke out against the Pearce Commission, going into exile in 1972. He continued his studies in, and then taught, Law in the United States. Acted as legal advisor to ZANU. Joined the struggle in Mozambique in 1972 as Deputy Secretary for Publicity and Information. Since independence he has held several ministerial posts.

Zimunya, Musaemura

(1949–) Zimbabwean poet and university teacher. Amongst his better known works are *Thought Tracks* (1982), *Kingfisher, Jikinya and Other Poems* (1983), *Country Dawns and City Lights* (1985).

THE WORLD

Achebe, Chinua

(1930–) Nigerian author, poet and novelist, known for his realistic description of life in Nigeria and his penetrating view of politicians, missionaries, civil servants and the corruption, superstition and prejudices found in society. His first novel, *Things Fall Apart* (1958), was the first major work by a black African writer to achieve international recognition. It was followed by *No Longer at Ease* (1960), *Arrow of God* (1964) and *A Man of the People* (1966). In 1972 he published *Beware Soul-Brother*, a volume of poems for which he won the Commonwealth Poetry Prize. Recently, *Anthills of the Savannah* (1987) was short-listed for the Booker Prize.

Aeschylus

(525–456BC) Playwright who is ranked, with Euripides and Sophocles, as one of the foremost dramatists of Ancient Greece. He wrote about 70 plays, of which seven survive, the most well-known being the three 'Story of Orestes' plays, namely *Agamemnon*, the *Libation Bearers* and the *Eumenides*.

Aesop

(620?–560BC?) Writer of fables who was probably a Greek slave. The fables, which include such famous stories as 'The Shepherd Boy and the Wolf' and 'The Goose that Laid the Golden Eggs', all have a moral message and are still printed and read throughout the world.

Alexander the Great

(356–323BC) King of Macedonia who was a pupil of Aristotle. He united the city-states of Ancient Greece and made great journeys of conquest over much of the Middle East, as far as the borders of India, creating the largest empire in the world at the time. He founded the city of Alexandria in Egypt and spread Greek culture and learning over much of the ancient world.

Amin, Field Marshal Idi Dada

(1926–) Exiled Ugandan dictator. He had a rapid rise in the army, becoming commander in 1966. Overthrew Milton Obote and became President in 1971, instituting rule of terror. Expelled Asians from Uganda in 1972. President of the OAU, 1975. His prestige was severely dented by successful raid by Israeli forces in 1975 to rescue hijack hostages at Entebbe airport. Overthrown in 1978 in Tanzanian-backed coup, he escaped and is believed to be living in Saudi Arabia.

Amundsen, Roald

(1872–1928) Norwegian explorer who in 1911 became the first person to reach the South Pole. He also navigated the North-West Passage through North America. He died during a rescue expedition in the Arctic.

Antony, Mark

(82–30BC) A Roman Consul at the time of the reign of Julius Caesar who, after Caesar's assassination, became part of the triumvirate that ruled Rome. He later commanded the eastern part of the Roman empire. While attempting to extend control over the empire by pursuing the Egyptian Queen Cleopatra, he was defeated by Octavian (later known as Augustus Caesar) and committed suicide.

Aquinas, St Thomas

(1225–1274) Italian theologian whose work became the basis for many doctrines of the Roman Catholic Church. His work was greatly influenced by the Greek philosopher, Aristotle. His writings *Summa contra Gentiles* and *Summa Theologica* contain his ideas on his system of theology. He is known as the Father of Moral Philosophy.

Arafat, Yasser (Mahammed Abed Ar'ouf Arafat)

(1929–) President of the State of Palestine and Chairman of the Palestine Liberation Organization (PLO). Born in Jerusalem, he did an engineering degree at Cairo university. Joined the League of Palestinian Students in 1944. Became their President in 1952, a position he held until 1956 when he formed Al Fatah (the Palestine National Liberation Movement). Became Chairman of the PLO in 1968. He has campaigned internationally for the liberation of Palestine from Israel and the official recognition of the State of Palestine, of which he was declared President in 1989.

Archimedes

(287–212BC) Greek mathematician and inventor who is best known for being the first to discover how to measure density. He proved the theory, now known as the 'Archimedes Principle', that a body placed in water will displace an equal volume of water. He also invented the 'Archimedes screw', a spiral pump for raising water.

Aristotle
(384–322BC) Greek philosopher and scientist who was a student of Plato and became tutor to Alexander the Great. He lectured on government and ethics and laid the foundations for the study of psychology. He established the Peripatetic School in Athens (so called because of his habit of pacing up and down while teaching).

Armstrong, Neil
(1930–) American astronaut who was part of the crew of 'Apollo XI' and, on 20 July 1969, became the first human being to set foot on the moon. As he stepped on to the moon surface he said: 'That's one small step for a man, one giant leap for mankind.'

Atahualpa
(1500?–1533) Last Emperor of the Inca empire in South America before the arrival of the Spanish invaders led by Francisco Pizarro. The invaders conquered the Incas and put Atahualpa to death.

Attila
(406?–453) Leader of the Huns who conquered much of eastern and central Europe. He had a reputation for being very fierce. His campaign in France and Italy met with failure and he was forced to retreat back to the River Danube, where he died during his wedding celebrations.

Augustus Caesar
(63BC–AD14) The first Roman Emperor, who assumed power in 27BC. Formerly known as Octavian, he expanded the Roman empire north and east. The empire reached a peak during his reign in terms of peace and artistic accomplishment. Among those who lived during his reign was Virgil.

Austen, Jane
(1775–1817) English writer whose novels, based on life among the Georgian English middle class, are considered masterpieces. Among her best-known books are *Pride and Prejudice, Sense and Sensibility, Emma* and *Northanger Abbey*.

Bach, Johann Sebastian
(1685–1750) German composer of classical music and a great organist who is known as the Father of Modern Music. His famous religious compositions include the *Mass in B Minor* and *The Passion according to St Matthew*. Among his well-known instrumental works are the *Brandenburg Concertos*.

Bacon, Francis
(1561–1626) English philosopher and politician best remembered for his essays. He is known as the Father of Experimental Philosophy. He had a great interest in the acquisition of knowledge and planned (but did not complete) an encyclopaedia of all knowledge.

Baldwin, James Arthur
(1924–85) Black American writer born in Harlem. He grew up in a background of poverty, racialism and religious fanaticism. His first novel *Go Tell it on the Mountain* (1953) describes religious conversion and the strong desire to escape from poverty and prejudice. Known for his defence of all types of minority and his determination to fight injustice. Other works include *Giovanni's Room* (1956), plays and collected essays, notably *The Fire Next Time* (1963).

Balzac, Honore de
(1799–1850) French author who wrote about eighty novels, including the well-known *Old Goriot*. His novels form what he called *Comedie Humaine (The Human Comedy)* and featured over 2000 characters who were intended to portray every type of person of his time.

Beckett, Samuel
(1906–) Irish novelist, playwright and poet, born in Dublin. Winner of the 1969 Noble Prize for Literature. His work is a philosophical meditation on the absurdity and meaninglessness of human life. *Waiting for Godot* (1952) and *Krapp's Last Tape* (1959) are his best-known plays: they capture the anguish, anxiety and despair of the isolated individual. His novels, *Molloy* (1951), *Malone Dies* (1951) and *The Unnameable* (1952), are portraits of human uncertainty. *Endgame* (1957) and other works confirm Beckett as one of the most influential of contemporary European writers.

Beethoven, Ludwig van
(1770–1827) German composer of classical music who was fired with revolutionary ideals. His famous *Eroica* symphony was originally dedicated to Napoleon as the liberator of Europe. He began to go deaf when he was about 30 but subsequently composed some of the world's greatest symphonies, concertos and sonatas.

Bellow, Saul
(1915–) Canadian-born American author, brought up in Chicago. Winner of the 1975 Nobel Prize for Literature. His first novel, *Dangling Man* (1944), describes the condition of modern man waiting, a hypersensitive passive victim of life. This theme dominates his work: *The Victim* (1948), *The Adventures of Augie March* (1953), *Henderson, The Rain King* (1959), *Herzog* (1961) and *Humboldt's Gift* (1975).

Bhutto, Benazir
(1955–) Prime Minister of Pakistan and first woman to head a Moslem Government. Daughter of Zulfidar Ali Bhutto, founder of the Pakistan People's Party (PPP) which had a policy of democracy and socialism. He was President from 1971 to 1973, then Prime Minister from 1973 to 1977, when he was ousted in a military coup by General Zia ul-Haq and subsequently executed for conspiring to kill a political opponent. Benazir became leader of the PPP on his death and continued actively to oppose General Zia, despite imprisonment and exile. Elected Prime Minister in December, 1988.

Bishop, Maurice
(1944–1983) Grenadian lawyer and politician. Leader of the New Jewel

Movement (Joint Endeavour for Welfare Education and Liberation). Elected Prime Minister in 1979 he endeavoured to bring greater democracy and equality into the processes of government. Assassinated in 1983.

Blake, William

(1757–1827) English Romantic poet, philosopher and artist who illustrated many books, including his own works and Dante's *Divine Comedy*. His poems and illustrations have a distinct haunting quality. Among his works are the two volumes of poetry entitled *Songs of Innocence*.

Boccaccio, Giovanni

(1313–1375) Italian novelist and poet who is known as the Father of the Novel. His most famous work is the *Decameron*, a collection of humorous tales about people isolated in Florence during the Plague. His works were a source of inspiration to prose writers throughout Europe.

Bolivar, Simon

(1783–1830) Powerful Latin American military leader and statesman, known as The Liberator. Fought for Colombia, Ecuador and Venezuela during their independence struggles against the Spanish settlers. He became President of Colombia.

Brahms, Johannes

(1833–1897) German composer of classical music whose work has a powerful dramatic quality. His well-known compositions include four symphonies, two piano concertos, a violin concerto, Hungarian dances and many songs.

Braille, Louis

(1809–1852) Frenchman who was blinded at the age of three and who developed the system of reading and writing now known as Braille. His system used raised points that could be read with the fingertips and thus opened up a new means of communication for the blind.

Brandt, Willy

(1913–) West German politician. Winner of the Nobel Peace Prize in 1971. Chairman of the Social Democratic Party (1964–1987), and Chancellor (1969–1974). Known for his involvement in development issues, including the Brandt Commission report, 'North-South: Co-operation for World Recovery', dealing with the problems of the Third World. Also known for his role in promoting disarmament.

Brecht, Bertolt

(1898–1956) German poet and playwright. His works set out to expose the hypocrisy of bourgeois values, war, chauvinism, militarism and greed. They always transcend the didactic because of his sympathy for human weaknesses and his understanding of the complexity of society. His works include *Drums in the Night* (1922), *The Threepenny Opera* (1929), *Mother Courage* (1939), *The Good Woman of Setzuan* (1953) and *The Caucasian Chalk Circle* (1949). His seven volumes of poems are now considered his best work.

Bronte, Charlotte

(1816–1855) English novelist who, with her sisters, Emily and Anne, wrote at a time when women were not considered capable of such talent. Her most famous novel is *Jane Eyre* (1847), which was followed by *Shirley* (1849) and *Villette* (1852). Her work is realistic, based on her own experiences and displays remarkable powers of observation and a deep concern for the position of women as independent and intelligent.

Buddha (Gautama)

(*c*.563–*c*.483BC) Nepalese philosopher and teacher of peace and enlightenment who founded the religion called Buddhism. He was the son of a rich man but gave up his wealth because he was overcome by the poverty and unhappiness of the masses. Often referred to as the Light of Asia.

Bush, George

(1924–) President of the United States of America. A self-made millionaire, he first entered politics as a conservative Republican in 1964 but, despite several attempts, was not elected. In 1971 he became US Ambassador to the UN, the first of a series of senior government positions, which included posting in China and being head of the Central Intelligence Agency. Became Vice-President under Ronald Reagan in 1980 and won the presidential campaign in 1988.

Caesar, Julius

(102–44BC) Roman emperor who as a general had conquered France and invaded Britain. He introduced the calendar used by most of the world today, naming the seventh month, July, after himself. His growing power as emperor led to his assassination in the Senate on 15 March, known as the Ides of March.

Calvin, John

(1509–1564) French-born Swiss theologian who developed a strict (puritanical) form of the Protestant religion. This form put faith and devout behaviour above doing good deeds for other people. Calvinism is still evident in some modern Protestant churches.

Carroll, Lewis

(1832–1898) English author of children's stories, who was born Charles Dodgson. His best-known book is *Alice in Wonderland*, in which the heroine, based on the daughter of a friend, has a dream in which she meets such characters as the White Rabbit, the Cheshire Cat and the Mad Hatter.

Caruso, Enrico

(1873–1921) Italian operatic tenor who is regarded as one of the greatest opera singers the world has known. He performed in many countries and had a repertoire of over 40 operas.

Castro, Fidel

(1926–) Cuban revolutionary leader who, following an unsuccessful attack on the Batista dictatorship in 1953 and two years imprisonment, led a small band of guerillas into Cuba from Mexico. Finally defeated the government in 1959 and became the President of Cuba. Continually harrassed by the USA (e.g. the abortive Bay of Pigs invasion in 1961), Cuba developed close ties with the Soviet Union and established a socialist state. Castro has sent Cuban soldiers to bolster liberation movements in many areas of Latin America and Africa, including Angola.

Catherine the Great

(1729–1796) Empress of Russia, officially referred to as Catherine II. Her armies extended Russia's borders to include Poland, the Crimea and Siberia.

Cervantes, Miguel de

(1547–1616) Spanish author whose most famous work, *Don Quixote*, is considered one of the world's greatest novels. He also wrote plays and poems.

Cezanne, Paul

(1839–1906) French impressionist painter who made much use of cubic, conical and spherical shapes in his works. His distinct style influenced the Cubist movement among European painters.

Charlemagne

(742–814) Founder of the Holy Roman Empire in 800, he was also known as Charles the Great. This empire covered most of central and western Europe. He did much to promote education and Christianity in his empire and became the most powerful figure of his time in Europe.

Chaucer, Geoffrey

(*c*.1340–1400) English poet who is known as the Father of English Poetry. His most famous work is *The Canterbury Tales*, in which a group of pilgrims tell each other tales as they proceed to Canterbury.

Chekov, Anton

(1860–1904) Russian author and playwright whose works revolve around the theme of loneliness. His famous short stories include *The Party* and *Ward No 6*. Among his well-known plays are *The Cherry Orchard* and *Uncle Vanya*.

Chiang, Kai-Shek

(1887–1975) Chinese general. As commander of the army from 1925, he tried to unite China but he was more anxious to defeat communism. He ruthlessly suppressed trade union and communist organizations. His nationalist government from 1928–37 unified most of China and reasserted traditional values. But there was constant war during this period and he was finally forced to resign. He left for Taiwan in 1949. The administration he established there is still known as the Republic of China.

Chopin, Frederic

(1810–1849) Polish composer of classical music who was a child prodigy. He became famous in Vienna and later lived in Paris. His works were mainly for piano, and included concertos, etudes, mazurkas, nocturnes and polonaises.

Churchill, Sir Winston

(1874–1965) British politician and writer. Prime Minister during the Second World War whose inspiring leadership contributed significantly towards the Allies' victory over Germany. Later came to regard Soviet communism as a threat and coined the phrase of the 'Iron Curtain' drawn across Europe. Defeated in 1945, he again became Prime Minister in 1951, until his resignation in 1955. Writings include a history of the English-speaking people. He won the Nobel Prize for Literature in 1953.

Cicero, Marcus

(106–43BC) Roman statesman, orator and writer whose work is some times seen as the height of Latin prose. He opposed Mark Antony's desire to rule Rome and was sentenced to death. He was killed trying to escape.

Cleopatra

(69–30BC) Egyptian queen who became the mistress of Julius Caesar and later of Mark Antony. After Antony's defeat by Augustus Caesar she committed suicide (apparently by placing a deadly snake on her body) to avoid being taken to Rome as a captive.

Columbus, Christopher

(1451–1506) Italian sailor and explorer who, on his voyage in 1492 to find a sea route from Europe to Asia, landed in the West Indies. His discovery of the Americas, till then an unknown continent to Europeans, led the way for the Spanish invasions of South and Central America.

Confucius

(551–479BC) Chinese philosopher whose teachings stressed the importance of moral behaviour, such as the need for kindness, wisdom and respect for elders. This philosophy became the cornerstone of Chinese society. His sayings were published in a book entitled *Confucian Analects*.

Conrad, Joseph

(1857–1924) Polish sea captain and writer who became a British subject in 1896. He developed an outstanding command of English and wrote several novels, often with experiences of the sea as a theme. His best-known books are *Heart of Darkness* and *Lord Jim*.

Copernicus, Nicolas

(1473–1543) Polish astronomer who is known as the Father of Modern Astronomy. His theory that the sun, not the earth, was the centre of the solar system contradicted the beliefs at the time. His theories were published in 1530 in his book *De Revolutionibus Orbium Coelestium*.

Cortes, Hernando

(1485–1547) Spanish explorer who conquered the Aztecs of South America and captured Mexico for Spain. He became the governor of Mexico and spread Spanish influence in central America.

Curie, Marie

(1867–1934) Polish-French physicist who discovered radium, polonium and the nature of radio-activity. Joint winner with her husband of the Nobel Prize for Physics in 1903, she was the first woman to win the Prize.

also first woman to hold a chair (Physics) at the Sorbonne University. In 1911 she was also the first person to win a second Nobel Prize, this time for Chemistry. Died as result of radiation to which she had been exposed during her work.

Da Gama, Vasco

(c.1469–1525) Portuguese sailor whose voyage to India around the southern coast of Africa in 1497–98 led to the start of the spice trade between the East Indies and Portugal. As a result of his voyage Portuguese colonies were set up in the Mozambique region.

Dante, Alighieri

(1265–1321) Italian poet who is perhaps the greatest Italian literary figure. His best-known work is the *Divine Comedy*, an imaginative summary of human history which describes the narrator's visions of hell and heaven. It was illustrated by William Blake.

Darwin, Charles

(1809–1882) British naturalist who in 1859 published *The Origin of Species by Means of Natural Selection.* This work expounded the theory of evolution for the first time and led to much controversy. He had arrived at this theory as a result of his observations on his voyage in 1831–1836 aboard the *HMS Beagle* to South America and the Galapagos Islands.

David

(c.?–c.973BC) Second king of Israel and the son of Saul. He became famous for slaying Goliath, a Philistine giant. He was a poet and harpist and composed many psalms. His reign was troubled by rebellions. He married Bathsheba and was succeeded by his son, Solomon.

Da Vinci, Leonardo

(1452–1519) Italian scientist, inventor, engineer, painter and sculptor who among other things designed a flying machine and wrote extensively on botany and astronomy. His famous paintings, *The Last Supper* and *Mona Lisa*, were painted in 1498 and 1503.

Dias, Bartolomew

(c.1457–1500) Portuguese sailor who reached the Cape of Good Hope in 1488. His voyage led to the opening up of a new sea route from Europe to East and eventually to the colonization of southern Africa.

Dickens, Charles

(1812–1870) English novelist whose books give a graphic description of life in 19th century England during a period of rapid industrialization and urbanization, and which particularly highlight the plight of the poor. Among his most famous works are *Pickwick Papers, David Copperfield, A Tale of Two Cities, Great Expectations* and *A Christmas Carol*.

Dostoevsky, Feodor

(1821–1881) Russian novelist whose works tell of human suffering. He was accused of political conspiracy and imprisoned for some time in Siberia. His most famous works are *The Brothers Karamazov* and *Crime and Punishment*.

Drake, Sir Francis
(c.1540–1596) English admiral who sailed around the world in 1577–1580 in the *Golden Hind*. In 1588 he successfully commanded the British fleet against the attempted invasion of England by the Spanish Armada.

Earhart, Amelia
(1897–1937?) American aviator who was the first woman to fly solo across the Atlantic (1932) and Pacific (1935) oceans. After further flying feats, she disappeared over the Pacific while on an attempted round-the-world flight.

Einstein, Albert
(1879–1955) German mathematical physicist who achieved world fame for his Theory of Relativity and numerous other discoveries in modern physics. While lecturing in California in 1930, he decided to stay on in the US after Hitler's rise to power. He persuaded the United States government to begin work on the atom bomb but urged control on use of atomic weapons. He won the Nobel Prize for Physics in 1921.

Eliot, George
(1819–80) (Real name was Mary Anne Evans) English novelist, intellectual and free-thinker. Amongst her works are *Adam Bede* (1859), *Mill on the Floss* (1860), *Silas Marner* (1861), *Middlemarch* (1871) and *Daniel Deronda* (1876). Her novels portray, with deep insight, the provincial life of the time and the gap between human aspiration and achievement.

Elliot, T(homas) S(tearns)
(1888–1965) American-born British poet, critic and dramatist who won the Nobel Prize for Literature in 1948. Among his best-known poems are 'The Love Song of Alfred J Prufrock', 'The Waste Land' and 'The Hollow Men'; his verse dramas include 'Murder in the Cathedral' (1935).

Elizabeth I
(1533–1603) English queen during whose reign Britain became a great sea power. She encouraged world exploration and British expansion. She is referred to as 'The Virgin Queen' because she never married.

Engels, Friedrich
(1820–1895) German socialist revolutionary who worked with Karl Marx on *The Communist Manifesto*. He also edited Marx's *Das Kapital* (1885). These works formed the basis of communist ideology. After fleeing to Britain, he wrote *The Condition of the Working Class in England*.

Ericson, Leif
(c.1000) Norse sailor and explorer who is credited with the 'discovery' of North America, four centuries before Christopher Colombus. He sailed westwards from Norway and reached what may have been either Labrador or Newfoundland on the east coast of North America.

Euclid
(c.400BC) Greek mathematician who has been called the most successful textbook writer of all time. He founded the school of mathematics in

Alexandria and his main work, entitled *Elements*, is still used as a geometry textbook.

Faulkner, William
(1897–1962) American novelist, born in Mississippi and known for his intensely emotive depiction of society in decay in the Deep South. Winner of the Nobel Prize for Literature in 1949. His novels include *Soldier's Pay* (1926), *The Sound and The Fury* (1929), *As I Lay Dying* (1930), *Absalom, Absalom!* (1936) and *Intruder in the Dust* (1948).

Francis of Assisi, St
(*c.*1181–1226) Italian priest who in 1209 founded the Roman Catholic Franciscan Order, based on a belief in chastity, poverty and obedience. He travelled throughout Europe propounding his beliefs and devoting himself to the care of the poor and the sick.

Freud, Sigmund
(1856–1939) Austrian doctor and founder of modern psychology who believed that the unconscious mind governs human behaviour. He investigated the significance of dreams and the importance of infantile experiences on behaviour. Among his greatest works was *The Interpretation of Dreams*.

Gagarin, Yuri
(1934–1968) Russian cosmonaut who on 12 April 1961 became the first man in space. He made the 89-minute journey in a 'Vostok' space satellite. Killed when testing a plane.

Galileo, Galilei
(1564–1642) Italian astronomer and mathematician whose observations confirmed Copernicus' theory that the earth revolves around the sun, but for this he was excommunicated from the Roman Catholic Church. Perfected the refracting telescope and discovered the law of the pendulum.

Gandhi, Indira
(1917–1984) Indian stateswoman. Daughter of Jawaharlal Nehru, she was imprisoned for wartime activities. She entered politics as an aide to her father, becoming Prime Minister from 1966 to 1977. In 1979 she was re-elected and ruled until her assassination by Sikh extremists in 1984.

Gandhi, Mohandas Karamchand
(1869–1948) Indian lawyer who led the mass movement that forced Britain to grant India independence in 1947. His campaign was based on passive resistance and civil disobedience. He also fought against racial discrimination in South Africa. Known as the 'Mahatma' ('Great Soul').

Gandhi, Rajiv
(1944–) Son of Indira Gandhi, whom he succeeded as Prime Minister on her assassination in 1984. Studied in India and England. Pilot with Indian Airlines before entering politics and becoming Minister in his mother's cabinet. Preceded Robert Mugabe as chairman of the Non-Aligned Movement.

Gauguin, Paul
(1848–1903) French artist, forerunner of the expressionists. A stockbroker by profession, he first painted as a hobby but gave up his job in 1883 and became full-time painter in Britanny. In 1891 rejected western civilization and went to live and paint in Tahiti. Known for his expansive use of colour and free form.

Gaulle, Charles de
(1890–1970) French general and statesman. President of France 1959–1969. Refused to surrender to Hitler in 1940 and fled to Britain to lead the Free French. Provisional President (1945–1946), he retired following political disagreement. He re-entered public life during the 1958 Algerian crisis, and drew up a new constitution: the Fifth Republic (1959) with himself as President. Student uprising in Paris in May 1968 shook his government and he resigned in 1969.

Genghis, Khan
(1167–1227) Mongolian leader and military genius who invaded China and conquered parts of the Middle East. His grandson, Kublai Khan, founded the Mongol dynasty in China.

Geronimo
(1829–1909) Apache Indian chief who resisted the white settlers in North America and moved his people from Arizona to Mexico rather than go into an Indian reserve. He surrendered in 1886 and he and his tribe were sent to Oklahoma, where he died.

Golding, William
(1911–) English writer. Winner of the Nobel Prize for Literature in 1983. His works include *Lord of the Flies* (1954), *The Inheritors* (1955), *The Spire* (1964), *The Pyramid* (1967), *Darkness Visible* (1979) and *Rites of Passage* (1980). His novels explore in fable form the view that evil is the basis of life and human motivation.

Goethe, Johann
(1749–1832) German poet and writer who initiated the romantic and modern movements in German literature. His novels include *The Sorrows of Young Werther,* while his play *Faust* is considered as one of the greatest works in western literature.

Grass, Günter
(1927–) German author, born in Danzig. He has written novels, poetry, essays, speeches and a play. A highly inventive writer, he uses grotesque images and events, mixing historical details with fantasy to evoke the needs of individuals in society. Achieved international fame with his first novel, *The Tin Drum* (1959), an epic treatment of Nazism and modern German history. Other works include *Dog Years* (1963) and *The Flounder* (1978).

Greene, Graham
(1904–) Writer born in England but widely travelled. His books have been centred in South America, Africa, Europe and the Far East. A left-

wing Catholic convert, his works explore the meaning of morality and his view of the squalid seediness of evil, and of man rescued from evil by the grace of God. His books include *Brighton Rock* (1938), *The Power and the Glory* (1940), *The Heart of the Matter* (1948), *The Quiet American* (1955) and *The Comedians* (1966).

Hadrian
(76–138) Roman emperor who improved the Roman empire's fortifications, drew up a legal code and extended the Roman empire eastwards to the Euphrates River. He visited Britain where he supervised the building of Hadrian's Wall across northern Britain.

Haile Selassie I
(1892–1975) Last Ethiopian emperor, who was deposed by a military coup in 1974. He claimed descent from King Solomon and the Queen of Sheba.

Hammerskjöld, Dag
(1905–61) Swedish diplomat and Secretary-General of the United Nations (1953–61). Used his position to help achieve peace in the Middle East, Laos, Lebanon and the Congo. In trying to find a solution to the Congo crisis, he was killed in a mysterious plane crash in Zambia and was posthumously awarded the Nobel Peace Prize.

Hammurabi
(1870–1750BC) Ruler of the Babylonian empire during its period of great growth and prosperity. He established a legal code which became known as the Code of Hammurabi.

Handel, George
(1685–1759) German composer of classical music who later lived in Britain. He became very popular in his life-time and wrote some 40 operas. He also composed many works for royal occasions, including the famous *Water Music*. His best-known religious work is the *Messiah*.

Hannibal
(247–183BC) Carthaginian general who fought the Romans in Spain and then led an army through the Alps to Rome, using elephants as beasts of burden. He became the leader of Carthage but when faced with capture by the Romans committed suicide.

Hardy, Thomas
(1840–1928) British novelist and poet who was one of the most popular writers of his time. Among his famous novels are *Tess of the D'Urbervilles*, *Far from the Madding Crowd* and *The Mayor of Casterbridge*.

Haydn, Joseph
(1732–1809) Austrian composer of classical music who established musical forms that influenced many later composers. Under the patronage of the Esterhazy family of Vienna he wrote many masses, operas and string quartets and over 100 symphonies.

Hegel, Georg
(1770–1831) German philosopher whose works had a great influence in

19th-century Europe. He integrated earlier philosophies into a system that stressed the historical sequence of philosophical ideas. Among his major works were the *Encyclopaedia of the Philosophical Sciences* and *Philosophy of Right*.

Hemingway, Ernest
(1899–1961) American author who mastered a simple prose style and whose works centred on the themes of moral values and physical courage. He was involved in the Spanish Civil War and in 1954 won the Nobel Prize for Literature. Among his famous books are *A Farewell to Arms, The Old Man and the Sea* and *For Whom the Bell Tolls*.

Henry VIII
(1491–1547) English king who had six wives, the divorce of the first, Catherine of Aragon, leading to England's break with the Roman Catholic Church and the establishment of the Church of England. His other wives were Anne Boleyn, Catherine Howard (both beheaded), Jane Seymour, Anne of Cleves and Catherine Parr. His daughter Elizabeth became Queen Elizabeth I.

Herodotus
(*c.*484–425BC) Greek historian and geographer known as the Father of History. He travelled throughout much of the Middle East and North Africa and wrote his great history of the Greeks and Persians which was in effect a history of the world as it was then known in Europe.

Hillary, Sir Edmund
(1919–) New Zealand mountain climber who, in 1953, accompanied by Sherpa Tensing, was the first person to reach the top of world's highest mountain, Mount Everest.

Hippocrates
(*c.*460–377BC) Greek physician who is known as the Father of Medicine. He practised surgery and was the first physician to show that diseases have natural causes. He formulated rules of conduct for doctors which became the basis of the Hippocratic Oath.

Hitler, Adolf
(1889–1945) Leader of German Nazi party and ruler of Germany from 1933 to 1945. He rearmed Germany and started the Second World War by invading Poland in 1939. He planned to conquer Europe, promote the Aryan race and exterminate Jews, as indicated in his book *Mein Kampf* ('My Struggle'). He was responsible for the murder of over six million Jews. When defeat was imminent he committed suicide.

Hobbes, Thomas
(1588–1679) English philosopher who wrote many works on the theme of government, based on the idea that humans are selfish and therefore need to be ruled by an all-powerful leader. His political theory was described in his famous work, *Leviathan*.

Ho Chi Minh
(1890–1969) Vietnamese socialist leader who led his country to independence from France after the Second World War and founded North

Vietnam. He then embarked on the struggle to unite North and South Vietnam, which was achieved in 1975 after his death.

Homer
(c.800BC) Greek writer and poet who is known as the Father of Poetry. His most famous epic poems, *The Iliad* and *The Odyssey*, tell the story of the Trojan War and of Odysseus' journey back from Troy to Greece.

Ibsen, Henrik
(1828–1906) Norwegian playwright who is known as the Father of Modern Drama. His plays are based on realism and deal with social problems. Among his best-known plays are *A Doll's House, Hedda Gabler* and *Peer Gynt*.

Ivan the Terrible
(1530–1584) First Czar of Russia, officially called Ivan IV. He expanded Russia northwards, made Moscow the capital city and earned his popular name because of his cunning and cruelty, which included killing his own son.

James, Henry
(1843–1916) American author and critic who explored the mores and sensibilities of wealthy middle-class Americans and Europeans. The psychology of human emotion and sexuality are minutely analysed in his novels, of which *The Portrait of a Lady* (1881) and *The Wings of a Dove* (1902) are the most widely read. Other writings include *What Maisie Knew* (1897), *The Turn of the Screw* (1898), *The Bostonians* (1886), *The Ambassadors* (1903), and *The Golden Bowl* (1904).

Joan of Arc, St
(1412–1431) French peasant girl who said she received divine commands to assist her country against the English. She led the French army to victory over the English at Orleans in 1429 (hence her popular name, 'The Maid of Orleans'). She was later imprisoned by the English, tried as a witch by the French and burned at the stake.

Joyce, James
(1882–1941) Irish novelist whose works are considered to be among the greatest masterpieces in the English language. Although he lived away fom Ireland after 1904, his books are set in Ireland and focus on the character of the Irish people. His most famous works include *A Portrait of the Artist as a Young Man, Finnegan's Wake, Dubliners* and *Ulysses*.

Jung, Carl Gustav
(1875–1961) Swiss psychologist who developed analytical psychology. Like Freud he stressed the importance of the unconscious mind and focused on childhood traumas when treating his patients. He was the first to identify people as being either 'introverts' or 'extroverts'.

Kafka, Franz
(1883–1924) Czech author, born in Prague. Writer of short stories, including *Metamorphisis* (1912), and three unfinished novels published posthumously: *The Trial* (1925), *The Castle* (1926) and *America* (1927).

Both a realist and a symbolist, Kafka evoked modern man's bewildered and alienated state of mind.

Keats, John
(1795–1821) English romantic poet whose most famous works include 'Endymion', 'Hyperion' and 'La Belle Dame sans Merci'. He was plagued by ill-health and died of tuberculosis in Italy.

Keller, Helen
(1880–1968) American lecturer and writer who was deaf and blind but through perseverance and the encouragement of her governess learned to speak, read and write. She devoted her life to working for the blind and published several books.

Kennedy, John Fitzgerald
(1917–1963) American Democratic politician and 35th President (1961–63). The youngest man, and first Catholic, to be elected president, 'JFK' brought new hope and enthusiasm to the office. He introduced domestic labour law reforms and civil rights improvements, but his presidency also saw the beginning of US military involvement in Vietnam. Assassinated in Dallas in 1963. His brother, Robert, ran for president in 1968 and was also assassinated.

Kenyatta, Jomo
(1890–1978) Former President of Kenya who led the fight for independence from Britain after the Second World War, resulting in his imprisonment. At Independence in 1963 he became Prime Minister, then President of the one-party state of Kenya, and by the 1970s had emerged as one of Africa's leading statesmen.

Khomeini, Ayatollah Ruhollah
(1900–1989) Iranian Shiite religious and political leader. Acclaimed an Ayatollah in 1950. Spent 16 years in exile, agitating for the overthrow of the Shah. Returned to Iran in 1979 and was proclaimed leader of the Islamic Revolution. Initiated the Iran–Iraq war. Shortly before his death, he issued a decree that Salman Rushdie be murdered for writing *The Satanic Verses*, a controversial book based on the life of Mohammed.

Khrushchev, Nikita
(1894–1971) Soviet statesman. First secretary of the Soviet Communist Party (1953–1964) and Prime Minister (1958–1964), Khrushchev was a close associate of Stalin and emerged as leader after Stalin's death. He built up enough support to launch an attack on Stalinism in 1956. During his years in power he instigated the notion of 'peaceful co-existence' and travelled widely. His quarrel with China and the failure of his economic policies finally led to his downfall.

King, Martin Luther
(1929–1968) American Baptist minister and leader of the black civil rights movement in the 1950s and 1960s. He believed in passive resistance and led many demonstrations, including a march on Washington. It was at this occasion that he said 'I have a dream' (of equality). He won the Nobel Peace Prize in 1964. Assassinated at a rally in Memphis.

Lavoisier, Antoine

(1743–1794) French scientist who is known as the Father of Modern Chemistry. He produced the first chemistry book, entitled *Elements of Chemistry*, wrote the first chemical equation and was the first person to give a scientific analysis of fire. An aristocrat, he was guillotined during the French Revolution.

Lawrence, D(avid) H(erbert)

(1885–1930) English writer of great importance and power. An idealist and free-thinker, his writings and paintings shocked contemporary society. Extremely honest, he refused to compromise his beliefs and used his creative talent to communicate those beliefs and feelings. Among his best-known novels are *Sons and Lovers* (1913), *The Rainbow* (1915), *Women in Love* (1920) and *Lady Chatterley's Lover* (1928).

Lenin, Vladimir Ilich

(1870–1924) Russian socialist revolutionary leader whose real name was Vladimir Ilich Ulyanov. He went to Europe in 1900 to set up the Social Democrat Workers' Party, became the Bolshevik leader and returned to Russia in 1905 to overthrow the Czar but was unsuccessful. He returned again in 1917 to lead the October Revolution, renamed the party the Communist Party and introduced Marxism to the Soviet Union.

Lindberg, Charles

(1902–1974) American aviator who in 1927 was the first person to fly solo non-stop across the Atlantic Ocean, taking 33-and-a-half hours. He promoted commercial and military aviation and his story was written in the book entitled *The Spirit of St Louis*.

Linnaeus, Carolus

(1707–1778) Swedish botanist who developed a system for classifying plants and animals according to genus and species. This system forms the basis for modern biological classification throughout the world.

Luther, Martin

(1483–1546) German Roman Catholic priest who broke with the Church in 1517, alleging that it was corrupt and questioning its authority. His teachings became the foundation of Lutheran and other Protestant denominations formed in Europe.

Luxemburg, Rosa

(1871–1919) Polish-German socialist feminist and pacifist, known as 'Red Rosa'. Writer, political activist and teacher, in 1912 she produced an economics textbook, *The Accumulation of Capital*. Imprisoned during World War I for her anti-war stand. Known for her dedication to the rights of workers, she was eventually arrested and murdered by police and soldiers.

Machiavelli, Niccolo

(1469–1527) Italian statesman and political writer whose most famous work was *The Prince*, a book on the art of practical politics. His belief was that the first consideration of a ruler was to be successful rather than moral, and that a ruler was justified in using any means to achieve an end and maintain authority.

Magellan, Ferdinand

(c. 1480–1521) Portuguese navigator who led the first expedition to sail round the world, leaving Spain in 1519 and sailing round South America into the Pacific Ocean. He was killed in the Philippines but one of the ships of his fleet of five continued and reached Spain in 1522.

Manley, Michael

(1924–) Jamaican politician who has become a charismatic leader representing the views of the poor people of the Third World. First came to prominence as organizer for the National Workers Union (1953–1955). In 1969 he became President of the People's National Party. Elected Prime Minister in 1972 on a socialist platform. Defeated in the 1980 elections, he was re-elected Prime Minister in 1989.

Mann, Thomas

(1875–1955) German author who was one of the greatest 20th-century novelists and short-story writers. He left Germany in 1933 when the Nazi party came to power. Among his best-known books are *Doctor Faustus, Death in Venice* and *The Magic Mountain*.

Mao Zedong (Tse-tung)

(1893–1976) Leader of the Chinese communist revolution who led his thousands of followers, mainly peasants, on the 'Long March' to northern China where he established a government. As leader of the Red Army he then fought against the Nationalist Chinese, defeating them in 1949, and became Chairman of the Communist Party and was head of China until his death. His socialist ideas were contained in his work, *The Thoughts of Chairman Mao*.

Marx, Karl

(1818–1883) German philosopher, economist and revolutionary who, with Engels, produced *The Communist Manifesto* (1848). He was forced to leave Germany and lived in Britain where he wrote *Das Kapital*, an analysis of capitalism that became the basis of the communist movement (first volume published 1867, the rest posthumously).

Mboya, Tom

(1930–1969) Kenyan politician. A trade union organizer, in 1960 he became leader of the Kenya Independence Movement, and founder member of the Kenya African National Union. After Kenyan independence in 1963, he held various senior posts. Assassinated in 1969.

Michelangelo

(1475–1564) Italian painter, sculptor and architect who is considered the greatest figure of the Italian Renaissance. Among his famous works are the frescoes on the ceiling of the Sistine Chapel in Rome, the chapel and tombs for the powerful Medici family, and his sculptures of David and of Mary attending the dead body of Jesus Christ, known as the 'Pieta'.

Milton, John

(1608–1674) English poet whose political and religious works show the 'grand style' of the English language at its height. His most famous epics, 'Paradise Lost' and 'Samson Agonistes', were written after he had become blind in 1652, hence his popular name, 'the Blind Poet'.

Mohammed (or Muhammad)
(c.570–c.632) Prophet and teacher who, as a result of divine visions, founded the Islamic religion, making Mecca the Islamic centre and preaching the worship of God, whom he called Allah. His teachings were written down and became the basis of the Holy Book of Muslims, known as the *Koran*.

Moi, Daniel Arap
(1924–) President of Kenya. Teacher from 1946–1956, he first entered politics in 1957, became a Minister in 1961, Vice-President in 1967 and succeeded Jomo Kenyatta as President in 1978.

Moses
(c.1300BC) Egyptian-born Hebrew leader who led his people from Egypt across the Red Sea to Palestine to escape persecution. During the journey he is said to have received the Ten Commandments from God on Mount Sinai and these became the basis of Hebrew law. He died before reaching Palestine.

Mozart, Wolfgang Amadeus
(1756–1791) Austrian composer of classical music who was a child prodigy. Among his operas, chamber music, concertos and 41 symphonies are the famous operas *Don Giovanni* and *The Magic Flute*, and the symphony No. 41 known as the *Jupiter*.

Mussolini, Benito
(1883–1945) Italian fascist dictator. Initially socialist, he supported Italian participation in World War I and organized radical right-wing groups which merged into the Fascist Party. Seized power in 1922. Violence, murder of political enemies and brilliant oratory as 'Il Duce' ('leader') gave him power. Invaded Ethiopia (1935), allied with Hitler (1936), and entered World War II in 1940. Deposed in 1943, he survived until 1945, when partisans shot him.

Naipaul, V(idiadhar) S(urajprasad)
(1932–) Trinidadian author. A *House for Mr Biswas* (1961) established him as a major novelist. A serious and comic satirist of life in Trinidad, England and Africa, his works include *The Mystic Masseur* (1957), *Mr Stone and the Knights Companion* (1963), *The Mimic Men* (1967) and *A Bend in the River* (1979).

Napoleon I
(1769–1829) Corsican-born military leader, known as 'the Little Corporal', who overthrew the government of France in 1799 and began to conquer Europe. He became Emperor of France but met a disastrous defeat in Russia in 1813. Returned to France in 1815 but was defeated by English and Prussian forces at Waterloo. Died in exile on St Helena.

Nasser, Gamal Abdel
(1918–1970) Former Egyptian President who led the revolt against King

Farouk in 1952. He took control of the Suez Canal in 1956 and adopted a militant stance towards Israel and the western powers. He brought about many reforms in Egypt.

Nebuchadnezzar

(c.600–562BC) Babylonian king who transformed Babylon into one of the most beautiful cities of the ancient world. He may have been responsible for the building of the famous Hanging Gardens of Babylon. Also remembered for destroying Jerusalem, making the Jews captive.

Nehru, Jawaharlal

(1889–1964) Indian leader of the independence movement who in 1947 became the first Prime Minister of independent India. A follower of Mahatma Gandhi, he was imprisoned nine times between 1921 and 1945 for his opposition to British rule. Held in high esteem at home and abroad, he formulated India's policy of neutrality and set up a state-controlled economy. Father of Indira Gandhi.

Newton, Sir Isaac

(1642–1727) English mathematician, astronomer and scientist whose work formed the basis of modern physical science. He studied the laws of gravity (inspired, it is said, by seeing an apple fall from a tree), discovered that sunlight is a mixture of colours, invented calculus and constructed the reflecting telescope. He published his findings on gravity in his greatest work, *Philosophiae Naturalis Principia Mathematica*.

Ngũgĩ wa Thiong'o

(1938–) Kenyan writer of international fame. A committed socialist, he believes that writers have a duty to expose the evils of society. Imprisoned by the Kenyan authorities for his play *Ngaahika Ndeenda* (I will Marry When I Want) in 1978 he was subsequently prevented from returning to his teaching post at the university and went into exile. Amongst his most well-known works are *Weep Not Child* (1964), *The River Between* (1965), *A Grain of Wheat* (1967), *Petals of Blood* (1967), *Devil on the Cross* (1978), *Detained* (1981) and *Matigari* (1989).

Nietzsche, Friedrich

(1844–1900) German philosopher and poet who criticized Christianity and searched for morality outside religion. Among his famous works are *Thus Spake Zarathustra* and *The Antichrist*.

Nightingale, Florence

(1820–1910) English philanthropist who directed nursing operations during the Crimean War, earning herself the name 'The Lady of the Lamp'. She revolutionized nursing care, introducing sanitary practices into hospitals and providing the basis of modern nursing procedures.

Nixon, Richard Milhaus

(1913–) US Republican politician and 37th President (1969–1974). Early career as lawyer included participation in anti-communist campaign by McCarthy. His success as president in improving US relations with China and in ending the Vietnam War (1973) was overshadowed by the

Watergate scandal, involving illegal efforts to ensure his re-election in 1972. Under threat of impeachment, Nixon became the first president to resign. Given free pardon by his successor, Gerald Ford.

Nkrumah, Kwame
(1909–1972) President of Ghana from 1960 to 1966, he led his country to independence from Britain in 1957. He was responsible for many social reforms and became a leading African statesman. In 1966, while visiting China, he was overthrown by the army and lived in exile in Guinea until his death. Leading advocate of African unity, writings include *Towards Colonial Freedom* (1947) and *Handbook of Revolutionary Warfare* (1968).

Nobel, Alfred
(1833–1896) Swedish scientist who in 1867 discovered how to make dynamite. From this and other inventions he became wealthy, but when he saw the use to which dynamite was being put in warfare he set up a fund from which annual cash prizes were to be awarded to people who made contributions to international peace, literature, physics, chemistry, medicine, physiology, and economics.

Nyerere, 'Mwalimu' Julius Kambarange
(1922–) Former President of Tanzania, who led his country to independence in 1961. Educated at Makerere and Edinburgh universities, he worked as a teacher, before he became MP in 1957. He introduced a concept of African socialism (Ujamaa) to Tanzania and in the 1970s developed many socialist programmes, e.g. nationalization of the banks and major industries. He also attempted to restructure the countryside in a national villagization programme. Consistent supporter of liberation movements in Southern Africa, his army helped overthrow Idi Amin's autocratic rule in Uganda. Retired as President in 1985 but remained chairman of the ruling party and of the South-South Commission.

Orwell, George (pseudonym of Eric Blair)
(1903–1950) English novelist and journalist, known for his powerful insights into the dangers inherent in totalitarian rule. *Animal Farm* (1945) and *Nineteen Eighty-Four* (1949) are among the most widely read books of this century. His other works include *Down and Out In Paris and London, Homage to Catalonia* and *Coming Up For Air*.

Ousmane, Sembene
(1923–) Senegalese novelist. A militant trade-unionist, his first book, *The Black Docker* (1956), is a vivid description of his own experiences as union leader. *God's Bits of Wood* (1960), a panoramic view of a strike, is a novel of protest. Marxist, humane and fair, he has a great gift for revealing the realities of the life of the poor and the oppressed.

Pankhurst, Emmeline
(1858–1928) Mother of English family of feminists, leaders of the Suffragette Movement. Emmeline and Christabel (1880–1958) founded the Women's Social and Political Union in 1903 and were militant activists. Both were often arrested and imprisoned for their views. The dedication and energy of this family – including also Sylvia (1882–1960)

and Adela (1885–1961) – made major contributions to the achievement of full women's voting rights.

Pasteur, Louis
(1822–1895) French scientist who developed pasteurization, a process that destroys bacteria in milk. He also advanced knowledge on immunity from disease and developed a vaccine against rabies.

Pericles
(c.490–429BC) Greek statesman whose strong support of the arts during his rule of the city state of Athens led to the period being known as the 'Age of Pericles'. He spread the idea of democracy throughout the Mediterranean world. He died of the plague during the Peloponnesian War against the Spartans.

Peter the Great
(1672–1725) Russian Czar who was officially known as Peter I. He expanded Russian influence westwards to Turkey and Persia and northwards to Sweden. He westernized his country, making it a leading European power, and founded the city of St Petersburg (now Leningrad) as the former capital of Russia.

Picasso, Pablo
(1881–1973) Spanish painter and sculptor who became world renowned for his cubist forms in art. He produced a prodigious number of paintings and drawings. Among the most well-known ones are 'Guernica', 'The Three Musicians' and 'Les Demoiselles d'Avignon'.

Plato
(c.427–347BC) Greek philosopher and pupil of Socrates who founded an academy which became the intellectual centre of Ancient Greece. His teachings were based on the belief that mind is more important than matter. In his famous work, *The Republic,* he wrote that the ideal state is one ruled by a philosopher king.

Polo, Marco
(c.1254–1324) Venetian who as a merchant made journeys to China and entered the diplomatic service of Kublai Khan. He returned to Venice 24 years later, and was the first European to bring back detailed knowledge of the 'Far East'.

Pythagoras
(c.500BC) Greek mathematician and philosopher who developed the Pythagorean theorem in geometry. He taught that numbers are central to all things and he may have been the first philosopher to believe that the earth was a sphere and that the planets do not stay in a fixed position.

Ramphal, Sir Shridath Surendranath
(1928–) Secretary-General of the Commonwealth from 1975 to 1989. Born in Europe and educated at King's College, London. Lawyer and politician in West Indies. He has helped give the Commonwealth a definite voice in international affairs, specially on developmental issues.

Rawlings, Jerry
(1947–) Head of State of Ghana. Educated at Achimota School and the Ghana Military Academy, he was a Flight Lieutenant in 1979 when he led a mutiny of junior officers for which he was briefly imprisoned. In 1979 he led a military coup and became head of the Armed Forces Revolutionary Council, but was later retired from the armed forces by the President. He returned as Head of State after another military coup in 1982, since when he has worked to improve the Ghanaian economy and stamp out corruption.

Rembrandt van Rijn
(1606–1669) Dutch painter who was one of the most productive artists in history, but died poor because he turned from painting wealthy merchants' portraits to painting dramatic scenes in which the individual was not paramount. His famous works include 'The Night Watch', 'The Prodigal Son' and 'Aristotle Contemplating the Bust of Homer'.

Renoir, Pierre Auguste
(1841–1919) Leading French impressionist painter whose subjects were mainly landscapes, flowers and children. Among his famous works are 'The Bathers' and 'The Luncheon of the Boating Party'.

Rodin, Auguste
(1840–1917) French impressionist sculptor whose work was influenced by Italian sculptors, including Michaelangelo. His realistic style became very influential in western art and among his many well-known statues are 'The Thinker', 'The Gates of Hell' and 'Saint John the Baptist'.

Roosevelt, Franklin Delano
(1882–1945) Became President of the USA in 1932. A Democrat, he instituted a vigorous 'New Deal' programme to support the unions, counter unemployment and improve labour relations. After the Japanese attack on Pearl Harbour in 1941, America became a British ally in World War II. He strongly advocated the need for a United Nations Organization but died before the UN was formed.

Rousseau, Jean Jacques
(1712–1778) French philosopher who believed that humans are basically good but are corrupted by socio-political institutions and that feelings are more important than reason. Among his famous writings is *The Social Contract*.

Rushdie, Salman
(1947–) Indian-born English author of *Midnight's Children* (1981), *Shame* (1983) and *The Satanic Verses* (1988). His books explore with rich satire and humour the worlds of the Indian subcontinent. *The Satanic Verses* provoked a death sentence on the author by Ayatollah Khomeini for blasphemy against Islam and Rushdie was forced into hiding.

Russell, Bertrand
(1872–1970) English philosopher and mathematician whose famous work *Principia Mathematica* laid the foundations of modern mathematics and logic. He wrote on many other subjects and in 1950 won the Nobel

Prize for Literature. He was twice imprisoned for his pacifist views and protested strongly against the use of nuclear weapons.

Sadat, Anwar
(1918–1981) Egyptian statesman. Colleague of Nasser in the Free Officers movement committed to independence. Took part in the coup that deposed King Farouk in (1952) and brought Nasser to power. Twice vice-president, became president on Nasser's death (1970). Known for his efforts to bring peace to the Middle East: winner of the Nobel Peace Prize in 1978 with Menachem Begin. Assassinated by Muslim extremists.

Salim, Salim Ahmed
(1942–) Tanzanian politician, born in Zanzibar; the new Secretary-General of the Organization of African Unity (1989). After diplomatic career with postings in Egypt, India and China, he became President of the UN Security Council and General Assembly. Within his own government, he has acted as both Minister of Defence and Prime Minister.

Schweitzer, Albert
(1875–1965) German philosopher and doctor who gained international recognition as an organist and spent much time in Africa as a missionary doctor. In 1913 he established a hospital in Lambarene in French Equatorial Africa where he treated thousands of patients. He won the Nobel Peace Prize in 1952 and used the money to establish a leper colony.

Senghor, Leopold Sedar
(1906–) African statesman and poet, President of Senegal (1959-1980). In 1946 he was elected to the French National Assembly as a Socialist Deputy and when Senegal became independent in 1959 he was elected President. He formulated the concept of 'negritude' which he defined as the 'sum total of the values of the African world'. Pan-Africanist, Marxist and Roman Catholic, his poetry includes *Songs in Shadow* (1945).

Shakespeare, William
(1546–1616) English playwright and poet whose plays are considered the greatest in the world in any language; 37 plays are attributed to him. Commonly referred to as 'the Bard of Avon', he worked as an actor and playwright at the Globe Theatre in London. Among his best-known plays are *A Midsummer Night's Dream, Hamlet, Macbeth, Romeo and Juliet* and *Othello*. [See page 145 for list of complete works.]

Shelley, Percy Bysshe
(1792–1822) English romantic poet and revolutionary whose works showed his hatred of tyranny and his belief in human perfectability. Among his famous poems are 'Ode to the West Wind' and 'To a Skylark'.

Smith, Adam
(1723–1790) Scottish economist whose famous work, *The Wealth of Nations,* argued that labour is the source of wealth and that an economy free of government control would produce the greatest good for the greatest number of people. He is known as the Father of the Science of Political Economy.

Socrates

(*c*.399–369BC) Greek philosopher who taught his pupils by asking them questions, a method known as the Socratic method. He developed ideas on what is right and wrong, but his ideas were not popular and he was accused of corrupting the youth, tried, found guilty and put to death by poisoning. Many of his teachings were recorded by Plato.

Solzhenitsyn, Alexander

(1918–) Russian novelist whose works exposed the worst aspects of the Stalin era. His criticism of Stalin led to imprisonment for eight years and exile in Siberia for three years. His novels *One Day in the Life of Ivan Denisovich* and *Cancer Ward* were among those that earned him the Nobel Prize for Literature in 1970. In 1973 he published *The Gulag Archipelago* in the west. For this he was expelled from the Soviet Union and was given asylum in the USA.

Sophocles

(*c*.496–406BC) Greek playwright who wrote over 100 plays, of which seven have survived. They are all tragedies in which the main characters meet their deaths heroically. His most well-known plays are *Electra, Antigone* and *Oedipus Rex.*

Soyinka, Wole

(1934–) Nigerian author and playwright who is a Professor of Drama and Literature. He has written many books and in 1986 was awarded the Nobel Prize for Literature. Among his works are *A Dance of the Forests, The Lion and the Jewel, The Man Died* (about his prison experience), *Ahe* (the story of his childhood) and *Myth, Literature and the African World.*

Stalin, Joseph

(1879–1953) Soviet leader, born J Dzhugashvili in Georgia. Expelled from theological studies for revolutionary activities, he joined the Bolsheviks under Lenin and, after imprisonment and exile during the Russian Revolution, became general secretary of the Communist Party in 1922. After Lenin's death, Stalin won a power struggle, ousting Trotsky and assuming full control by 1929. His rule was marked by the ruthless purges of the 1930s and the harsh enforcement of the collectivization of agriculture and industry. He rallied the armed forces during World War II, but his autocratic rule continued in the post-war years. He was finally exposed by Khrushchev in 1956.

Stevenson, Robert Louis

(1850-1894) Scottish author and poet who in his later years lived in Samoa where he became involved in the Samoan struggle for liberation. Among his famous works are *Treasure Island, Kidnapped, The Strange Case of Doctor Jekyll and Mr Hyde* and many poems for children collected in *A Child's Garden of Verses.*

Stowe, Harriet Beecher

(1811–1896) American author whose most famous work was *Uncle Tom's Cabin.* This anti-slavery novel contributed significantly to the debate on slavery, one of the issues of the American Civil War.

Tchaikovsky, Peter Ilich
(1840–1893) Russian composer of classical music who is among the most popular composers of all time. He wrote many operas, ballets and symphonies, his most famous works being *Swan Lake, The Nutcracker, Romeo and Juliet* and the *Pathetique* symphony.

Tereshkova, Valentina
(1937–) Russian cosmonaut who was the first woman in space. Her historic flight took place in June 1963 in the spacecraft 'Vostok VI', which made 48 orbits around the earth and was in space for over 70 hours.

Thatcher, Margaret
(1925–) British Conservative politician, the country's first woman Prime Minister (1979) and the first party leader to be re-elected to three terms in office. Known as the 'Iron Lady' for her toughness, her government has been noted for severe economic policies, privatization, curbing the trade unions and reducing the benefits of the welfare state.

Tito, Josip Broz
(1892–1980) Yugoslav statesman. As president for nearly 30 years (1953–1980), he maintained a socialist government that was independent. In 1937 he became secretary-general of the Yugoslav Communist Party. He organized successful resistance to Hitler and after the war became Prime Minister. In 1948 he refused to give in to pressure from Stalin and established a foreign policy of non-alignment.

Tolstoy, Leo
(1828–1910) Russian novelist who was born an aristocrat but gave up his wealth to live a simple and Christian life. The themes of social reform and non-violence were the essence of his famous works, *War and Peace* and *Anna Karenina*.

Touré, Sékou
(1922–1984) Guinean statesman and President (1958–1984). Active trade unionist, elected to French National Assembly in 1956. A convinced Marxist, he opposed de Gaulle's federal plans for French West African and at independence in 1958, broke all links with France.

Trotsky, Leon
(1897–1940) Russian revolutionary and theorist who led the people against forces opposed to the October Revolution of 1917. In the struggle for the leadership of Russia after Lenin's death he lost to Stalin, was banished and later murdered in Mexico.

Tshombe, Moise
(1919–1969) Congolese politician, Prime Minister of the Belgian Congo (now Zaire), he led the secession of Katanga province in 1960. Following UN intervention, he was forced to surrender in 1963 and went into exile. In 1964, he was recalled by President Kasavubu and became Prime Minister of the Congo, but was dismissed in 1965. Fled to Spain and in 1966 was accused of treason: kidnapped and taken to Algeria in 1967, he remained under house arrest until his death from a heart attack.

Tutankhamun

(c.1370–1335BC) Egyptian pharoah who restored traditional religion in Egypt and moved the capital to Thebes. His tomb in the Valley of the Kings was discovered in the 1920s and the treasures removed to Cairo Museum. These treasures were later exhibited around the world.

Twain, Mark

(1835–1910) American author whose real name was Samuel Clemens. His novels and stories for children, based mainly on his childhood memories of Missouri, made perceptive comments on American society. The most well-known works are *The Adventures of Tom Sawyer* and *The Adventures of Huckleberry Finn.*

Van Gogh, Vincent

(1853–1890) Dutch impressionist painter whose work was characterized by thick brushstrokes. He suffered from mental illness, as is evident in later paintings, and committed suicide. Among his most famous works were 'Self Portrait', 'The Starry Night' and 'Le Pont d'Arles'. His painting of yellow irises is one of the highest valued paintings in the world.

Verdi, Guiseppe

(1813–1901) Italian composer of classical music who was one of the most prestigious opera composers of all time. Among his well-known operas are *Falstaff, La Traviata, Rigoletto and Aida.* His best-known instrumental and choral work is his *Requiem.*

Verne, Jules

(1828–1905) French writer of science fiction whose work foresaw many 20th-century inventions. His best-known books are *Around the World in Eighty Days, Journey to the Centre of the Earth* and *Twenty Thousand Leagues Under the Sea.*

Victoria

(1819–1901) Longest reigning British monarch, during whose rule the British empire expanded into Asia and Africa. She became Empress of India and, with her husband Prince Albert, encouraged art and technological advance. The period during which she reigned is known in Britain as the Victorian Age.

Virgil

(70–19BC) Regarded as the greatest Latin poet. His real name was Publius Vergilius Maro. His best-known work is the *Aeneid,* an epic poem about Aeneas the Trojan, the legendary founder of Rome, and the growth and achievements of the Roman empire.

Voltaire

(1694–1778) One of the greatest French writers and philosophers of his time, whose real name was François Marie Arouet. His novels, plays and poetry challenged the established order and helped prepare the way for the French Revolution. His most famous novel is *Candide.*

Washington, George

(1732–1799) First President of the USA. A champion of American independence from Britain, of which America was a colony, he led the army against the British who were defeated in 1781 and America became a republic. President from 1789 to 1797.

Whitman, Walt

(1819–1892) American poet whose poems are considered to be distinctly American in style. In his works he praised America and democracy but condemned slavery. His volume of poems, entitled *Leaves of Grass*, is considered a literary classic.

Wordsworth, William

(1770–1850) English Romantic poet who sought to denounce artificiality and whose poems were mainly on the theme of the beauty of nature. His most famous poems include 'I Wandered Lonely as a Cloud', 'She Was a Phantom of Delight' and 'The Prelude'.

Xerxes

(c.519–465BC) Persian king who in 480BC invaded Greece with an army of 200 000 men. He won at Thermopylae but was later defeated at Salamis and Plateae. His invasion was the last attempt by the Persians to conquer the Greeks.

Zhou, En Lai (Chou En-Lai)

(1898–1976) Chinese revoluntionary, statesman, administrator and diplomat. He organized the revolt in Shangai in 1927 which was violently suppressed by Chiang Kai-shek. Became chief adviser to the Communist Party during the Chinese civil war. He formed a close partnership with Mao Tse-tung and, on the establishment of the People's Republic of China in 1949, became Prime Minister till his death. During the Cultural Revolution (1966–1968) he actively restrained extremists and helped restore order.

INVENTIONS AND INVENTORS

Aeroplane	Orville and Wilbur Wright (1903)
Airship	Ferdinand von Zeppelin (1900)
Algebra	Possibly an Arab, Alkhowarizni (825)
Anaesthetic	James Simpson (1847)
Antiseptics	Joseph Lister (1867)
Atlas	Gerhardus Mercator (1569)
Ball-point pen	John Loud (1888)
Barometer	Evangelista Torricelli (1643)
Bicycle	Kirkpatrick Macmillan (1838)
Bunsen burner	Robert Bunsen (1850)
Calculus (forerunner of computer)	Charles Babbage (1834)
Cash register	James Ritty (1879)
Chronometer	John Harrison (1735)
Cinema	Louis Lumiere (1895)
Clock, pendulum	Galilei Galileo/Christian Huygens (1600s)
Cotton gin	Eli Whitney (1793)
Diesel engine	Rudolf Diesel (1897)
Dynamite	Alfred Nobel (1867)
Dynamo	Michael Faraday (1831)

Electric motor	Michael Faraday (1821)
Gas lighting	William Murdock (1792)
Gunpowder	Roger Bacon (1240)
Gyroscope	Jean Foucault (1852)
Hovercraft	C. Cockerell (1955)
Internal combustion engine	Gottlieb Daimler (1883)
Jet engine	Frank Whittle (1930)
Kaleidoscope	David Brewster (1817)
Laser	Theodore Maiman (1960)
Lightning conductor	Benjamin Franklin (1752)
Macadam roads	John McAdam (1815)
Machine gun	Richard Gatling (1862)
Micrometer	William Gascoigne (1638)
Microscope	Zacharias Jansen (1590)
Morse Code	Samuel Finley Morse (1838)
Motor car	Karl Benz (1885)
Neon light	Georges Claude (1911)
Nylon	W. H. Carothers (1938)
Paper-making machine	Francois Robert (1798)
Penicillin	Alexander Fleming (1928)
Phonograph	Thomas Alva Edison (1877)
Photography	Joseph Niepce/Louis Daguerre (1826–1839)
Piano	Bartolomeo Cristofori (1709)
Postage stamps	Rowland Hill (1840)
Printing (from moveable type)	Johannes Gutenberg (1454)
Radar	Robert Watson-Watt (1935)
Radio-telescope	Karl Jansky (1931)
Radium	Marie and Pierre Curie (1898)
Revolver	Samuel Colt (1836)
Safety lamp	Sir Humphrey Davy (1815)
Sewing machine	Elias Howe (1845)
Spectacles	Alexander de Spina (1285)
Spinning frame	Richard Arkwright (1769)
Spinning jenny	James Hargreaves (1767)
Stainless steel	Henry Brearley (1914)
Steam engine	James Watt (1765)
Steam locomotive	Richard Trevithick (1803)
Steel converter	Henry Bessemer (1956)
Stethoscope	Rene Laennec (1816)
Telegraph, electric	Charles Wheatstone (1837)
Telephone	Alexander Graham Bell (1876)
Telescope, reflecting	Isaac Newton (1669)
Television	John Logie Baird (1926)
Thermometer	Galilei Galileo (1595)
Typewriter	Sholes and Gidden (1874)
Vaccination	Edward Jenner (1796)
Watch	Peter Henlein (1504)
Wireless	Guglielmo Marconi (1895)
X-ray tube	Wilhelm Rontgen (1895)

PART THREE

Continents & Nations of the World

CONTINENTS

The nations of the world are located on the six inhabited continents in the world. Two continents – the Arctic and the Antarctic – are uninhabitable although there are some scientific research stations on them. The list here gives the names of the continents, their size, their population and their population density:

Continent	Area	Population	Pop.density
Asia	44 060 000 sq km	2 814 000 000	168
Africa	30 340 000 sq km	518 000 000	44
North America	24 350 000 sq km	390 000 000	41
South America	17 830 000 sq km	260 000 000	36
Europe	10 520 000 sq km	680 000 000	166
Australasia	7 685 000 sq km	16 000 000	5

NATIONS

The list below of all the nations of the world gives their commonly used name and, in brackets, their official name. Zimbabwe is not included in the list because information about this country is given in more detail in *Part One: Facts about Zimbabwe.*

Afghanistan (Democratic People's Republic of Afghanistan)
In Asia, bordered by China, Pakistan, Iran and the Soviet Union
Area: 647 000 sq km
Population: 18 700 000
Capital: Kabul
Economy: Mainly agriculture; some mining and manufacturing
Currency: Afghani

Albania (People's Socialist Republic of Albania)
In Europe, bordered by Yugoslavia and Greece
Area: 29 000 sq km
Population: 2 950 000
Capital: Tirane
Economy: Mainly agriculture; some mining, forestry
Currency: Lek

Algeria (Democratic and Popular Republic of Algeria)
In Africa, bordered by Morocco, Sarahawi Arab Democratic Republic, Mauritania, Mali, Niger, Libya and Tunisia (independence 1962)
Area: 2 382 000 sq km
Population: 20 380 000
Capital: Algiers
Economy: Mainly agriculture; some mining and manufacturing
Currency: Dinar

Andorra (Principality of Andorra)
  In Europe, bordered by Spain and France
  Area: 450 sq km
  Population: 40 000
  Capital: Andorra
  Economy: Mainly tourism; some farming and mining
  Currency: French franc and Spanish peseta

Angola (People's Republic of Angola)
  In Africa, bordered by Congo, Zaïre, Zambia and Namibia
    (independence 1975)
  Area: 1 247 000 sq km
  Population: 7 630 000
  Capital: Luanda
  Economy: Mainly agriculture; some mining and oil production
  Currency: Kwanza

Antigua and Barbuda
  In the Caribbean Sea, north east of Venezuela
  Area: 440 sq km
  Population: 79 000
  Capital: St John's
  Economy: Mainly tourism; some farming and manufacturing
  Currency: East Caribbean dollar

Argentina (Republic of Argentina)
  In South America, bordered by Chile, Bolivia, Paraguay, Brazil and
  Uruguay
  Area: 2 777 000 sq km
  Population: 28 970 000
  Capital: Buenos Aires
  Economy: Mainly industry, agriculture and trade; some mining
  Currency: Austral

Australia (Commonwealth of Australia)
  In Pacific/Indian Ocean
  Area: 7 687 000 sq km
  Population: 16 248 800
  Capital: Canberra
  Economy: Mainly agriculture, mining and manufacturing
  Currency: Australian dollar

Austria (Republic of Austria)
  In Europe, bordered by Switzerland, Liechtenstein, West Germany,
    Czechoslovakia, Hungary, Yugoslavia and Italy
  Area: 84 000 sq km
  Population: 7 530 000
  Capital: Vienna
  Economy: Mainly manufacturing and trade; some agriculture, forestry
    and mining
  Currency: Schilling

Bahamas (Commonwealth of the Bahamas)
In the West Indies, south east of United States of America
Area: 14 000 sq km
Population: 240 000
Capital: Nassau
Economy: Mainly tourism
Currency: Bahama dollar

Bahrain (The State of Bahrain)
In the Persian Gulf, bordered by Saudi Arabia
Area: 622 sq km
Population: 400 000
Capital: Ali Manamah
Economy: Mainly oil production and refining; some fishing and manu-
facturing
Currency: Dinar

Bangladesh (People's Republic of Bangladesh)
In Asia, bordered by India and Burma
Area: 140 000 sq km
Population: 100 000
Capital: Dacca
Economy: Mainly agriculture; some industry
Currency: Taka

Barbados
In the West Indies, north east of Venezuela
Area: 430 sq km
Population: 260 000
Capital: Bridgetown
Economy: Mainly tourism and agriculture
Currency: Barbados dollar

Belgium (Kingdom of Belgium)
In Europe, bordered by Netherlands, West Germany, Luxembourg
and France
Area: 31 000 sq km
Population: 9 850 000
Capital: Brussels
Economy: Mainly industrial and commercial; some agriculture
Currency: Belgian franc

Belize
In Central America, bordered by Mexico and Guatemala
Area: 23 000 sq km
Population: 160 000
Capital: Belmopan
Economy: Mainly agriculture; some fishing and industry
Currency: Belize dollar

Benin (People's Republic of Benin; formerly Dahomey)
In Africa, bordered by Togo, Burkina Faso, Niger and Nigeria
(independence 1960)

Area: 113 000 sq km
Population: 3 800 000
Capital: Porto Novo
Economy: Mainly agriculture
Currency: C.F.A. franc

Bermuda
In Atlantic Ocean, off west coast of United States of America
Area: 53 sq km
Population: 60 000
Capital: Hamilton
Economy: Mainly tourism and agriculture
Currency: Bermuda dollar

Bhutan (Kingdom of Bhutan)
In Asia, bordered by China and India
Area: 47 000 sq km
Population: 1 500 000
Capital: Thimphu
Economy: Mainly agriculture; some mining
Currency: Ngultrum

Bolivia (Republic of Bolivia)
In South America, bordered by Brazil, Paraguay, Argentina, Chile and
    Peru
Area: 1 100 000 sq km
Population: 5 900 000
Capital: Sucre (official); La Paz (actual)
Economy: Mainly agriculture; some manufacturing and mining
Currency: Boliviano

Botswana (Republic of Botswana; formerly Bechuanaland)
In Africa, bordered by Namibia, Zimbabwe and South Africa
    (independence 1966)
Area: 600 000 sq km
Population: 950 000
Capital: Gaborone
Economy: Mainly agriculture and mining
Currency: Pula

Brazil (Federative Republic of Brazil)
In South America, bordered by Guiana, Surinam, Guyana, Venezuela,
    Colombia, Peru, Bolivia, Paraguay, Argentina and Uruguay
Area: 8 512 000 sq km
Population: 110 000 000
Capital: Brasilia
Economy: Mainly industry and agriculture
Currency: Cruzado

Bulgaria (People's Republic of Bulgaria)
In Europe, bordered by Romania, Turkey, Greece and Yugoslavia
Area: 111 000 sq km
Population: 9 000 000

Capital: Sofia
Economy: Mainly industry; some agriculture
Currency: Lev

Burkina Faso (formerly Upper Volta)
In Africa, bordered by Mali, Niger, Benin, Togo, Ghana and Ivory Coast (independence 1960)
Area: 274 000 sq km
Population: 7 400 000
Capital: Ouagadougou
Economy: Mainly agriculture
Currency: C.F.A. franc

Burma (Socialist Republic of the Union of Burma)
In Asia, bordered by China, Laos, Thailand, Bangladesh and India
Area: 678 000 sq km
Population: 37 600 000
Capital: Rangoon
Economy: Mainly agriculture and forestry; some mining
Currency: Kyat

Burundi (Republic of Burundi)
In Africa, bordered by Rwanda, Tanzania and Zaïre (independence 1962)
Area: 28 000 sq km
Population: 4 300 000
Capital: Bujumbura
Economy: Mainly agriculture; some industry
Currency: Burundi franc

Cameroon (United Republic of Cameroon)
In Africa, bordered by Chad, Central Africa Republic, Congo, Gabon, Equatorial Guinea and Nigeria (independence 1960)
Area: 475 000 sq km
Population: 9 100 000
Capital: Yaounde
Economy: Mainly agriculture
Currency: C.F.A. franc

Canada
In North America, bordered by United States of America
Area: 9 976 000 sq km
Population: 24 500 000
Capital: Ottawa
Economy: Mainly manufacturing and agriculture
Currency: Canadian dollar

Cape Verde Islands (Republic of Cape Verde)
In Atlantic Ocean, off coast of West Africa
Area: 4 000 sq km
Population: 340 000
Capital: Praia

Economy: Mainly agriculture and fishing; some mining
Currency: Cape Verde escudo

Central African Republic
In Africa, bordered by Chad, Sudan, Zaïre, Congo and Cameroon
   (independence 1960)
Area: 623 000 sq km
Population: 2 420 000
Capital: Bangui
Economy: Mainly agriculture; some mining and manufacturing
Currency: C.F.A. franc

Chad (Republic of Chad)
In Africa, bordered by Libya, Sudan, Central African Republic,
   Cameroon, Nigeria and Niger (independence 1960)
Area: 1 284 000 sq km
Population: 4 800 000
Capital: N'Djamena
Economy: Mainly agriculture
Currency: C.F.A. franc

Chile (Republic of Chile)
In South America, bordered by Peru, Argentina and Bolivia
Area: 757 000 sq km
Population: 11 700 000
Capital: Santiago
Economy: Mainly mining and manufacturing
Currency: Chilean peso

China (People's Republic of China)
In Asia, bordered by Soviet Union, Afghanistan, India, Nepal, Pakistan,
   Bhutan, Burma, Laos, Vietnam, North Korea and Mongolia
Area: 9 561 000 sq km
Population: 1 000 800 000
Capital: Beijing
Economy: Mainly agriculture; growing manufacturing industry
Currency: Renmimbi yuan

Colombia (Republic of Colombia)
In South America, bordered by Venezuela, Brazil, Peru, Ecuador and
   Panama
Area: 1 139 000 sq km
Population: 29 900 000
Capital: Bogota
Economy: Mainly agriculture; some mining and manufacturing
Currency: Colombian peso

Comoro Islands (Federal and Islamic Republic of the Comoros)
In the Indian Ocean, off coast of Mozambique
Area: 2 000 sq km
Population: 350 000
Capital: Moroni
Economy: Mainly agriculture
Currency: C.F.A. franc

Congo (People's Republic of the Congo)
In Africa, bordered by Cameroon, Central African Republic, Zaïre, Angola and Gabon (independence 1960)
Area: 342 000 sq km
Population: 1 600 000
Capital: Brazzaville
Economy: Mainly agriculture and forestry; some mining
Currency: C.F.A. franc

Costa Rica (Republic of Costa Rica)
In Central America, bordered by Nicaragua and Panama
Area: 51 000 sq km
Population: 2 400 000
Capital: San Jose
Economy: Mainly agriculture; some industry
Currency: Colon

Cuba (Republic of Cuba)
In West Indies, south of United States of America
Area: 115 000 sq km
Population: 10 300 000
Capital: Havana
Economy: Mainly agriculture and manufacturing
Currency: Cuban peso

Cyprus (Republic of Cyprus)
In the Mediterranean Sea, south of Turkey
Area: 9 000 sq km
Population: 650 000
Capital: Nicosia
Economy: Mainly tourism, agriculture, mining and manufacturing
Currency: Cyprus pound

Czechoslovakia (Czechoslovak Socialist Republic)
In Europe, bordered by Poland, the Soviet Union, Hungary, Austria, West Germany and East Germany
Area: 128 000 sq km
Population: 15 700 000
Capital: Prague
Economy: Mainly manufacturing; some agriculture
Currency: Koruna

Denmark (Kingdom of Denmark)
In Europe, bordered by West Germany
Area: 43 000 sq km
Population: 5 160 000
Capital: Copenhagen
Economy: Mainly manufacturing
Currency: Danish kroner

Djibouti (Republic of Djibouti; formerly Afars and Issas)
In Africa, bordered by Ethiopia and Somalia (independence 1977)

Area: 22 000 sq km
Population: 360 000
Capital: Djibouti
Economy: Mainly shipping and railway transportation
Currency: Djibouti franc

Dominica (Commonwealth of Dominica)
In the Caribbean Sea, north west of Venezuela
Area: 751 sq km
Population: 80 000
Capital: Roseau
Economy: Mainly agriculture, food processing, tourism and mining
Currency: East Caribbean dollar

Dominican Republic
On Hispaniola Island, in the Caribbean Sea
Area: 49 000 sq km
Population: 5 960 000
Capital: Santo Domingo
Economy: Mainly agriculture; some mining
Currency: Dominican peso

Ecuador (Republic of Ecuador)
In South America, bordered by Colombia and Peru
Area: 284 000 sq km
Population: 7 800 000
Capital: Quito
Economy: Mainly agriculture; some mining and manufacturing
Currency: Sucre

Egypt (Arab Republic of Egypt)
In Africa, bordered by Sudan, Libya and Israel (independence 1922)
Area: 1 001 000 sq km
Population: 43 000 000
Capital: Cairo
Economy: Mainly agriculture; some industry
Currency: Pound

El Salvador (Republic of El Salvador)
In Central America, bordered by Honduras and Guatemala
Area: 21 000 sq km
Population: 5 300 000
Capital: San Salvador
Economy: Mainly agriculture
Currency: Colon

Equatorial Guinea (Republic of Equatorial Guinea)
In Africa, bordered by Cameroon and Gabon (independence 1968)
Area: 28 000 sq km
Population: 400 000
Capital: Malabo
Economy: Mainly agriculture, forestry and fishing
Currency: Ekuele

Ethiopia

In Africa, bordered by Sudan, Djibouti, Somalia and Kenya
(independence 1941)
Area: 1 222 000 sq km
Population: 42 000 000
Capital: Addis Ababa
Economy: Mainly agriculture; some mining and industry
Currency: Ethiopian birr

Falkland Islands

In Atlantic Ocean, off coast of Argentina
Area: 12 000 sq km
Population: 2 500
Capital: Stanley
Economy: Mainly agriculture
Currency: Falklands pound

Fiji Islands

In Pacific Ocean, north east of Australia
Area: 18 000 sq km
Population: 680 000
Capital: Suva
Economy: Mainly agriculture; some tourism and manufacturing
Currency: Fiji dollar

Finland (Republic of Finland)

In Europe, bordered by the Soviet Union, Norway and Sweden
Area: 337 000 sq km
Population: 4 800 000
Capital: Helsinki
Economy: Mainly industry, agriculture, commerce and forestry
Currency: Markka

France (French Republic)

In Europe, bordered by Spain, Belgium, Luxembourg, West Germany,
Switzerland, Italy, Monaco and Andorra
Area: 547 000 sq km
Population: 54 400 000
Capital: Paris
Economy: Mainly industry and agriculture
Currency: Franc

French Guiana

In South America, bordered by Brazil and Surinam
Area: 91 000 sq km
Population: 75 000
Capital: Cayenne
Economy: Mainly mining and forestry
Currency: Franc

Gabon (Gabon Republic)

In Africa, bordered by Equatorial Guinea, Cameroon and Congo
(independence 1960)

Area: 266 000 sq km
Population: 958 000
Capital: Libreville
Economy: Mainly agriculture and forestry
Currency: C.F.A. franc

Gambia (The Gambia)
In Africa, bordered by Senegal (independence 1965)
Area: 11 000 sq km
Population: 660 000
Capital: Banjul
Economy: Mainly agriculture
Currency: Dalasi

Germany, East (German Democratic Republic)
In Europe, bordered by Poland, Czechoslovakia and West Germany
Area: 108 000 sq km
Population: 16 600 000
Capital: East Berlin
Economy: Mainly industry
Currency: Ostmark

Germany, West (Federal Republic of Germany)
In Europe, bordered by Denmark, Netherlands, East Germany, Czechoslovakia, Austria, Switzerland, France, Belgium and Luxembourg
Area: 248 000 sq km
Population: 61 500 000
Capital: Bonn
Economy: Mainly industry, commerce and agriculture
Currency: Deutsche mark

Ghana (Republic of Ghana)
In Africa, bordered by Burkina Faso, Togo and Ivory Coast (independence 1957)
Area: 239 000 sq km
Population: 12 600 000
Capital: Accra
Economy: Mainly agriculture; some mining
Currency: Cedi

Gibraltar
In Europe, bordered by Spain
Area: 6 sq km
Population: 30 000
Capital: Gibraltar
Economy: Mainly commerce and tourism
Currency: Gibraltar pound

Greece (Hellenic Republic)
In Europe, bordered by Bulgaria, Yugoslavia, Albania and Turkey
Area: 132 000 sq km

Population: 9 900 000
Capital: Athens
Economy: Mainly industry and agriculture
Currency: Drachma

Greenland
In north Atlantic Ocean
Area: 2 176 000 sq km
Population: 60 000
Capital: Godthaab
Economy: Mainly agriculture
Currency: Danish krone

Grenada (State of Grenada)
In the Caribbean Sea, north east of Venezuela
Area: 344 sq km
Population: 120 000
Capital: St George's
Economy: Mainly tourism, agriculture and fishing
Currency: East Caribbean dollar

Guadaloupe
In Caribbean Sea, north east of Venezuela
Area: 2 000 sq km
Population: 350 000
Capital: Pointe a Pitre
Economy: Mainly agriculture
Currency: Franc

Guatemala (Republic of Guatemala)
In Central America, bordered by Mexico, Honduras, Belize and El
   Salvador
Area: 109 000 sq km
Population: 7 980 000
Capital: Guatemala City
Economy: Mainly agriculture and industry
Currency: Quetzal

Guinea (Republic of Guinea)
In Africa, bordered by Guinea-Bissau, Senegal, Mali, Ivory Coast,
   Liberia and Sierra Leone (independence 1958)
Area: 246 000 sq km
Population: 5 440 000
Capital: Conakry
Economy: Mainly agriculture and mining; some commerce
Currency: Syli

Guinea-Bissau (Republic of Guinea-Bissau)
In Africa, bordered by Senegal and Guinea (independence 1974)
Area: 36 000 sq km
Population: 700 000
Capital: Bissau
Economy: Mainly agriculture
Currency: Peso

Guyana (Co-operative Republic of Guyana)
  In South America, bordered by Surinam, Brazil and Venezuela
  Area: 215 000 sq km
  Population: 850 000
  Capital: Georgetown
  Economy: Mainly agriculture and mining
  Currency: Dollar

Haiti (Republic of Haiti)
  On Hispaniola Island, in Caribbean Sea
  Area: 28 000 sq km
  Population: 6 760 000
  Capital: Port-au-Prince
  Economy: Mainly tourism and agriculture
  Currency: Gourde

Honduras (Republic of Honduras)
  In Central America, bordered by Nicaragua, El Salvador and Guatemala
  Area: 112 000 sq km
  Population: 4 000 000
  Capital: Tegucigalpa
  Economy: Mainly agriculture; some mining and manufacturing
  Currency: Lempira

Hong Kong
  In South-East Asia, bordered by China
  Area: 1 000 sq km
  Population: 5 400 000
  Capital: Hong Kong
  Economy: Mainly commerce and manufacturing
  Currency: Hong Kong dollar

Hungary (Hungarian People's Republic)
  In Europe, bordered by Czechoslovakia, the Soviet Union, Romania,
    Yugoslavia and Austria
  Area: 93 000 sq km
  Population: 10 900 000
  Capital: Budapest
  Economy: Mainly industry; some agriculture
  Currency: Forint

Iceland (Republic of Iceland)
  In north Atlantic Ocean
  Area: 103 000 sq km
  Population: 240 000
  Capital: Reykjavik
  Economy: Mainly fishing and fish processing; some manufacturing
    and agriculture
  Currency: Icelandic krona

India (Republic of India)
In Asia, bordered by China, Nepal, Bhutan, Bangladesh, Burma and Pakistan
Area: 3 287 000 sq km
Population: 740 000 000
Capital: New Dehli
Economy: Mainly agriculture; some manufacturing and mining
Currency: Indian rupee

Indonesia (Republic of Indonesia)
Between Indian and Pacific Oceans
Area: 1 907 000 sq km
Population: 156 000 000
Capital: Jakarta
Economy: Mainly agriculture; some manufacturing
Currency: Rupiah

Iran (Islamic Republic of Iran)
In Asia, bordered by the Soviet Union, Afghanistan, Pakistan, Iraq and Turkey
Area: 1 648 000 sq km
Population: 40 800 000
Capital: Tehran
Economy: Mainly agriculture and oil production
Currency: Rial

Iraq (Republic of Iraq)
In Asia, bordered by Turkey, Iran, Kuwait, Saudi Arabia, Jordan and Syria
Area: 435 000 sq km
Population: 14 000 000
Capital: Baghdad
Economy: Mainly oil production and agriculture
Currency: Iraqi dinar

Ireland (Republic of Ireland)
In Europe, bordered by Northern Ireland
Area: 70 000 sq km
Population: 3 600 000
Capital: Dublin
Economy: Mainly industry; some agriculture
Currency: Punt

Israel (State of Israel)
In Asia, bordered by Lebanon, Syria, Jordan and Egypt
Area: 21 000 sq km (excluding occupied area of 90 000 sq km)
Population: 4 160 000 (excluding population in occupied area)
Capital: Jerusalem
Economy: Mainly manufacturing and commerce; some agriculture
Currency: Shekel

Italy (Italian Republic)
In Europe, bordered by Switzerland, Austria, Yugoslavia and France
Area: 301 000 sq km
Population: 58 000 000
Capital: Rome
Economy: Mainly commerce, manufacturing and agriculture
Currency: Lira

Ivory Coast (Republic of the Ivory Coast)
In Africa, bordered by Mali, Burkina Faso, Ghana, Liberia and Guinea
(independence 1960)
Area: 322 000 sq km
Population: 9 178 000
Capital: Abidjan
Economy: Mainly agriculture, forestry and fishing
Currency: C.F.A. franc

Jamaica
In the Caribbean Sea, north of Colombia
Area: 11 000 sq km
Population: 2 300 000
Capital: Kingston
Economy: Mainly agriculture, manufacturing, mining and tourism
Currency: Jamaican dollar

Japan
In Pacific Ocean, off the east coast of Asia
Area: 372 000 sq km
Population: 120 200 000
Capital: Tokyo
Economy: Mainly manufacturing and commerce
Currency: Yen

Jordan (Hashemite Kingdom of Jordan)
In Asia, bordered by Syria, Iraq, Saudi Arabia and Israel
Area: 98 000 sq km
Population: 2 600 000
Capital: Amman
Economy: Mainly agriculture; some industry
Currency: Jordanian dinar

Kampuchea (Democratic Kampuchea)
In Asia, bordered by Thailand, Laos and Vietnam
Area: 181 000 sq km
Population: 8 300 000
Capital: Phnom Penh
Economy: Mainly agriculture
Currency: Riel

Kenya (Republic of Kenya)
In Africa, bordered by Sudan, Ethiopia, Somalia, Tanzania and Uganda
(independence 1963)
Area: 564 000 sq km
Population: 17 200 000

Capital: Nairobi
Economy: Mainly agriculture and tourism; some manufacturing
Currency: Kenya shilling

Kiribati (Republic of Kiribati)
In Pacific Ocean, north east of New Guinea
Area: 719 sq km
Population: 60 000
Capital: Tarawa
Economy: Mainly agriculture; some mining
Currency: Australian dollar

Korea, North (Democratic People's Republic of Korea)
In Asia, bordered by China, Soviet Union and South Korea
Area: 121 000 sq km
Population: 19 400 000
Capital: Pyongyang
Economy: Mainly manufacturing and mining; some agriculture
Currency: Won

Korea, South (Republic of Korea)
In Asia, bordered by North Korea
Area: 98 000 sq km
Population: 39 300 000
Capital: Seoul
Economy: Mainly manufacturing and agriculture
Currency: Won

Kuwait (State of Kuwait)
In Asia, bordered by Iraq and Saudi Arabia
Area: 18 000 sq km
Population: 1 600 000
Capital: Kuwait
Economy: Mainly oil production
Currency: Kuwaiti dinar

Laos (Lao People's Democratic Republic)
In Asia, bordered by China, Vietnam, Kampuchea, Thailand and Burma
Area: 237 000 sq km
Population: 4 000 000
Capital: Vientiane
Economy: Mainly agriculture
Currency: New kip

Lebanon (Republic of Lebanon)
In Asia, bordered by Syria and Israel
Area: 10 000 sq km
Population: 2 600 000
Capital: Beirut
Economy: Mainly commerce, agriculture and industry
Currency: Lebanese pound

Lesotho (Kingdom of Lesotho)
  In Africa, bordered by South Africa (independence 1966)
  Area: 30 000 sq km
  Population: 1 500 000
  Capital: Maseru
  Economy: Mainly agriculture
  Currency: Maluti

Liberia (Republic of Liberia)
  In Africa, bordered by Guinea, Ivory Coast and Sierra Leone
    (independence 1847)
  Area: 111 000 sq km
  Population: 2 200 000
  Capital: Monrovia
  Economy: Mainly mining and agriculture
  Currency: Liberian dollar

Libya (People's Socialist Libyan Arab Jamahiriya)
  In Africa, bordered by Egypt, Sudan, Chad, Niger, Algeria and Tunisia
    (independence 1951)
  Area: 1 760 000 sq km
  Population: 3 200 000
  Capital: Tripoli
  Economy: Mainly oil production
  Currency: Libyan dinar

Liechtenstein (Principality of Liechtenstein)
  In Europe, bordered by Austria and Switzerland
  Area: 157 sq km
  Population: 30 000
  Capital: Vaduz
  Economy: Mainly industry and agriculture
  Currency: Swiss franc

Luxembourg (Grand Duchy of Luxembourg)
  In Europe, bordered by Belgium, West Germany and France
  Area: 3 000 sq km
  Population: 380 000
  Capital: Luxembourg
  Economy: Mainly mining and agriculture
  Currency: Luxembourg franc

Macao
  In South East Asia, bordered by China
  Area: 16 sq km
  Population: 320 000
  Capital: Macao
  Economy: Mainly commerce
  Currency: Pataca

Madagascar (Democratic Republic of Madagascar; formerly Malagasy
  Republic)
  In Indian Ocean, off coast of Mozambique (independence 1960)
  Area: 587 000 sq km

Population: 9 300 000
Capital: Antananarivo
Economy: Mainly agriculture; some mining and industry
Currency: Franc

Malawi (Republic of Malawi; formerly Nyasaland)
In Africa, bordered by Zambia, Mozambique and Tanzania (independence 1964)
Area: 118 000 sq km
Population: 6 450 000
Capital: Lilongwe
Economy: Mainly agriculture
Currency: Kwacha

Malaysia
In Asia, bordered by Thailand and Singapore
Area: 330 000 sq km
Population: 14 600 000
Capital: Kuala Lumpur
Economy: Mainly agriculture; some mining and manufacturing
Currency: Ringgit

Maldive Islands (Republic of Maldives)
In Indian Ocean, south west of India
Area: 297 sq km
Population: 160 000
Capital: Male
Economy: Mainly fishing
Currency: Rufiyaa

Mali (Republic of Mali)
In Africa, bordered by Algeria, Niger, Burkina Faso, Ivory Coast, Guinea, Senegal and Mauritania (independence 1960)
Area: 1 240 000 sq km
Population: 7 500 000
Capital: Bamako
Economy: Mainly agriculture
Currency: C.F.A. franc

Malta (Republic of Malta)
In western Mediterranean Sea
Area: 316 sq km
Population: 380 000
Capital: Valletta
Economy: Mainly shipbuilding; some tourism and agriculture
Currency: Maltese pound

Martinique
In Caribbean Sea, north east of Venezuela
Area: 1 102 sq km
Population: 360 000
Capital: Fort-de-France
Economy: Mainly tourism and agriculture
Currency: Franc

Mauritania (Islamic Republic of Mauritania)
   In Africa, bordered by Sarahawi Republic, Algeria, Mali and Senegal
      (independence 1960)
   Area: 1 031 000 sq km
   Population: 1 800 000
   Capital: Nouakchott
   Economy: Mainly agriculture; some industry and mining
   Currency: Ouguiya

Mauritius
   In the Indian Ocean, east of Madagascar
   Area: 2 000 sq km
   Population: 1 020 000
   Capital: Port Louis
   Economy: Mainly sugar industry and tourism
   Currency: Mauritian rupee

Mexico (United Mexican States)
   In North America, bordered by United States of America, Belize and
      Guatemala
   Area: 1 973 000 sq km
   Population: 74 500 000
   Capital: Mexico City
   Economy: Mainly agriculture; some oil industry and manufacturing
   Currency: Mexican peso

Monaco (Principality of Monaco)
In Europe, bordered by France
   Area: 1,5 sq km
   Population: 27 000
   Capital: Monaco
   Economy: Mainly tourism
   Currency: French franc

Mongolia (Mongolian People's Republic)
   In Asia, bordered by the Soviet Union and China
   Area: 1 565 000 sq km
   Population: 1 800 000
   Capital: Ulan Bator
   Economy: Mainly agriculture; some industry
   Currency: Tugrik

Morocco (Kingdom of Morocco)
   In Africa, bordered by Algeria and Sarahawi Republic (independence
      1956)
   Area: 445 000 sq km
   Population: 22 200 000
   Capital: Rabat
   Economy: Mainly agriculture and commerce
   Currency: Dirham

Mozambique (People's Republic of Mozambique)
In Africa, bordered by Zimbabwe, Tanzania, Swaziland, Malawi and
South Africa (independence 1975)
Area: 783 000 sq km
Population: 12 900 000
Capital: Maputo
Economy: Mainly agriculture; some industry
Currency: Metical

Namibia
In Africa, bordered by South Africa, Botswana, Zambia and Angola
(independence 1989)
Area: 824 000 sq km
Population: 1 050 000
Capital: Windhoek
Economy: Mainly mining
Currency: Rand

Nauru Islands (Republic of Nauru)
In Pacific Ocean, east of Australia
Area: 21 sq km
Population: 9 000
Capital: none (people live in coastal villages)
Economy: Mainly mining
Currency: Australian dollar

Nepal (Kingdom of Nepal)
In Asia, bordered by China and India
Area: 141 000 sq km
Population: 14 980 000
Capital: Kathmandu
Economy: Mainly agriculture; some industry
Currency: Nepalese rupee

Netherlands, The (Kingdom of the Netherlands)
In Europe, bordered by West Germany and Belgium
Area: 41 000 sq km
Population: 14 440 000
Capital: Amsterdam
Economy: Mainly manufacturing and commerce
Currency: Guilder

New Zealand
In Pacific Ocean, south east of Australia
Area: 269 000 sq km
Population: 3 200 000
Capital: Wellington
Economy: Mainly manufacturing and agriculture
Currency: New Zealand dollar

Nicaragua (Republic of Nicaragua)
  In Central America, bordered by Honduras and Costa Rica
  Area: 130 000 sq km
  Population: 2 990 000
  Capital: Managua
  Economy: Mainly agriculture; some industry and commerce
  Currency: Cordoba

Niger (Republic of Niger)
  In Africa, bordered by Algeria, Libya, Chad, Nigeria, Benin, Burkina
    Faso and Mali (independence 1960)
  Area: 1 267 000 sq km
  Population: 5 800 000
  Capital: Niamey
  Economy: Mainly agriculture
  Currency: C.F.A. franc

Nigeria (Federal Republic of Nigeria)
  In Africa, bordered by Niger, Cameroon, Chad and Benin (independence
    1960)
  Area: 924 000 sq km
  Population: 94 750 000
  Capital: Lagos
  Economy: Mainly agriculture and oil production
  Currency: Naira

Norway (Kingdom of Norway)
  In Europe, bordered by Sweden, Finland and the Soviet Union
  Area: 324 000 sq km
  Population: 4 120 000
  Capital: Oslo
  Economy: Mainly manufacturing
  Currency: Norwegian krone

Oman (Sultanate of Oman)
  In Asia, bordered by United Arab Emirates, Yemen (Aden) and Saudi
    Arabia
  Area: 300 000 sq km
  Population: 990 000
  Capital: Muscat
  Economy: Mainly agriculture and oil industry
  Currency: Rial omani

Pakistan (Islamic Republic of Pakistan)
  In Asia, bordered by Iran, Afghanistan, China and India
  Area: 888 000 sq km
  Population: 103 000 000
  Capital: Islamabad
  Economy: Mainly agriculture; some manufacturing
  Currency: Pakistan rupee

Panama (Republic of Panama)
  In Central America, bordered by Colombia and Costa Rica
  Area: 76 000 sq km
  Population: 2 030 000
  Capital: Panama City
  Economy: Mainly agriculture and transportation
  Currency: Balboa

Papua New Guinea
  On the island of New Guinea, in the Pacific Ocean
  Area: 462 000 sq km
  Population: 3 350 000
  Capital: Port Moresby
  Economy: Mainly agriculture; some manufacturing and mining
  Currency: Kina

Paraguay (Republic of Paraguay)
  In South America, bordered by Brazil, Argentina and Bolivia
  Area: 407 000 sq km
  Population: 3 390 000
  Capital: Asunción
  Economy: Mainly agriculture; some manufacturing
  Currency: Guarani

Peru (Republic of Peru)
  In South America, bordered by Ecuador, Colombia, Brazil, Bolivia and
    Chile
  Area: 1 285 000 sq km
  Population: 19 350 000
  Capital: Lima
  Economy: Mainly agriculture, fishing, manufacturing and mining
  Currency: Inti

Philippines (Republic of Philippines)
  In Pacific Ocean, south east of China
  Area: 300 000 sq km
  Population: 51 600 000
  Capital: Manila
  Economy: Mainly agriculture; some manufacturing and mining
  Currency: Peso

Poland (Polish People's Republic)
  In Europe, bordered by the Soviet Union, Czechoslovakia and East
    Germany
  Area: 313 000 sq km
  Population: 36 480 000
  Capital: Warsaw
  Economy: Mainly industry and manufacturing
  Currency: Zloty

Portugal (Portuguese Republic)
  In Europe, bordered by Spain
  Area: 92 000 sq km

Population: 10 280 000
Capital: Lisbon
Economy: Mainly mining, manufacturing, agriculture and fishing
Currency: Escudo

Puerto Rico
In Caribbean Sea, north of Venezuela
Area: 9 000 sq km
Population: 2 980 000
Capital: San Juan
Economy: Mainly agriculture and fishing
Currency: US dollar

Qatar (State of Qatar)
In Asia, bordered by Saudi Arabia and the United Arab Emirates
Area: 12 000 sq km
Population: 240 000
Capital: Doha
Economy: Mainly oil production; some agriculture
Currency: Riyal

Romania (Socialist Republic of Romania)
In Europe, bordered by the Soviet Union, Bulgaria, Yugoslavia and
   Hungary
Area: 238 000 sq km
Population: 22 880 000
Capital: Bucharest
Economy: Mainly agriculture, manufacturing and mining
Currency: Leu

Rwanda (Republic of Rwanda)
In Africa, bordered by Uganda, Tanzania, Burundi and Zaïre
   (independence 1962)
Area: 26 000 sq km
Population: 5 480 000
Capital: Kigali
Economy: Mainly agriculture; some mining
Currency: Franc

Saint Christopher-Nevis
In the Caribbean Sea, north of Venezuela
Area: 357 sq km
Population: 65 000
Capital: Basseterre
Economy: Mainly agriculture and tourism
Currency: East Caribbean dollar

Saint Lucia
In the Caribbean Sea, north of Venezuela
Area: 616 sq km
Population: 140 000
Capital: Castries
Economy: Mainly agriculture
Currency: East Caribbean dollar

Saint Vincent and the Grenadines
In the Caribbean Sea, north of Venezuela
Area: 388 sq km
Population: 130 000
Capital: Kingstown
Economy: Mainly agriculture, fishing, manufacturing and tourism
Currency: East Caribbean dollar

San Marino (The Most Serene Republic of San Marino)
In Europe, bordered by Italy
Area: 61 sq km
Population: 20 000
Capital: San Marino
Economy: Mainly agriculture and tourism; some manufacturing
Currency: Italian lira

São Tomé and Principé (Democratic Republic of São Tomé and Principé)
In Atlantic Ocean, west of Gabon
Area: 964 sq km
Population: 90 000
Capital: São Tomé
Economy: Mainly agriculture and fishing
Currency: Dobra

Sarahawi Republic (formerly Western Sahara)
In Africa, bordered by Morocco, Algeria and Mauritania (independence 1976)
Area: 266 000 sq km
Population: 110 000
Capital: El Aaiun
Economy: Mainly agriculture
Currency: Spanish peseta

Saudi Arabia (Kingdom of Saudi Arabia)
In Asia, bordered by Jordan, Kuwait, Iraq, Qatar, United Arab Emirates, Oman, Yemen (Sana) and Yemen (Aden)
Area: 2 150 000 sq km
Population: 9 180 000
Capital: Riyadh
Economy: Mainly oil production and agriculture
Currency: Riyal

Senegal (Republic of Senegal)
In Africa, bordered by Mauritania, Mali, Gambia, Guinea and Guinea-Bissau (independence 1960)
Area: 196 000 sq km
Population: 6 140 000
Capital: Dakar
Economy: Mainly agriculture, commerce and mining
Currency: C.F.A. franc

Seychelles (Republic of Seychelles)
  In Indian Ocean, east of Kenya
  Area: 376 sq km
  Population: 70 000
  Capital: Victoria
  Economy: Mainly tourism; some fishing
  Currency: Rupee

Sierra Leone (Republic of Sierra Leone)
  In Africa, bordered by Guinea and Liberia (independence 1961)
  Area: 72 000 sq km
  Population: 4 080 000
  Capital: Freetown
  Economy: Mainly agriculture and mining
  Currency: Leone

Singapore (Republic of Singapore)
  In Asia, south of Malaysia
  Area: 581 sq km
  Population: 2 980 000
  Capital: Singapore
  Economy: Mainly commerce and manufacturing
  Currency: Dollar

Solomon Islands
  In Pacific Ocean, north east of Australia
  Area: 28 000 sq km
  Population: 260 000
  Capital: Honiara
  Economy: Mainly agriculture, fishing and forestry
  Currency: Dollar

Somalia (Somali Democratic Republic)
  In Africa, bordered by Djibouti, Kenya and Ethiopia (independence
    1960)
  Area: 638 000 sq km
  Population: 6 400 000
  Capital: Mogadishu
  Economy: Mainly agriculture
  Currency: Shilling

South Africa (Republic of South Africa)
  In Africa, bordered by Namibia, Botswana, Zimbabwe, Lesotho,
    Swaziland and Mozambique
  Area: 1 221 000 sq km
  Population: 28 480 000
  Capital: Pretoria (administrative), Cape Town (legislative)
  Economy: Mainly manufacturing and mining; some agriculture
  Currency: Rand

Soviet Union (Union of Soviet Socialist Republics; also commonly
referred to as Russia)
In Asia, bordered by Norway, Finland, Poland, Czechoslovakia,
Hungary, Romania, Turkey, Iran, Afghanistan, China, Mongolia and
North Korea
Area: 22 402 000 sq km
Population: 274 000 000
Capital: Moscow
Economy: Mainly agriculture and industry
Currency: Rouble

Spain (Spanish State)
In Europe, bordered by France, Andorra and Portugal
Area: 505 000 sq km
Population: 38 700 000
Capital: Madrid
Economy: Mainly agriculture and manufacturing
Currency: Peseta

Sri Lanka (Democratic Socialist Republic of Sri Lanka)
In Indian Ocean, south east of India
Area: 66 000 sq km
Population: 15 650 000
Capital: Colombo
Economy: Mainly agriculture and mining
Currency: Rupee

Sudan (Democratic Republic of the Sudan)
In Africa, bordered by Egypt, Ethiopia, Kenya, Uganda, Zaïre, Central
African Republic, Chad and Libya (independence 1956)
Area: 2 506 000 sq km
Population: 20 300 000
Capital: Khartoum
Economy: Mainly agriculture
Currency: Pound

Surinam (Republic of Surinam)
In South America, bordered by French Guiana, Brazil and Guyana
Area: 163 000 sq km
Population: 470 000
Capital: Paramaribo
Economy: Mainly mining; some agriculture
Currency: Guilder

Swaziland (Kingdom of Swaziland)
In Africa, bordered by South Africa and Mozambique (independence
1968)
Area: 17 000 sq km
Population: 610 000
Capital: Mbabane
Economy: Mainly agriculture and mining
Currency: Lilangeni

Sweden (Kingdom of Sweden)
In Europe, bordered by Finland and Norway
Area: 450 000 sq km
Population: 8 380 000
Capital: Stockholm
Economy: Mainly manufacturing and commerce
Currency: Krona

Switzerland (Swiss Confederation)
In Europe, bordered by West Germany, Austria, Liechtenstein, Italy
and France
Area: 41 000 sq km
Population: 6 500 000
Capital: Berne
Economy: Mainly agriculture, commerce, manufacturing and tourism
Currency: Franc

Syria (Syrian Arab Republic)
In Asia, bordered by Turkey, Iraq, Jordan, Israel and Lebanon
Area: 185 000 sq km
Population: 8 880 000
Capital: Damascus
Economy: Mainly agriculture, commerce and industry
Currency: Pound

Taiwan (Republic of China)
In Pacific Ocean, east of China
Area: 36 000 sq km
Population: 18 800 000
Capital: Taipei
Economy: Mainly manufacturing
Currency: Dollar

Tanzania (United Republic of Tanzania)
In Africa, bordered by Kenya, Uganda, Mozambique, Malawi, Zambia,
Rwanda, Burundi and Zaïre (independence 1961)
Area: 945 000 sq km
Population: 20 700 000
Capital: Dar es Salaam
Economy: Mainly agriculture; some mining
Currency: Shilling

Thailand (Land of the Free)
In Asia, bordered by Laos, Kampuchea, Malaysia and Burma
Area: 514 000 sq km
Population: 50 000 000
Capital: Bangkok
Economy: Mainly agriculture and manufacturing; some mining
Currency: Baht

Togo (Republic of Togo)
In Africa, bordered by Burkina Faso, Benin and Ghana (independence 1957)
Area: 56 000 sq km
Population: 2 810 000
Capital: Lomé
Economy: Mainly agriculture; some mining
Currency: C.F.A. franc

Tonga Islands (Kingdom of Tonga)
In Pacific Ocean, south east of Fiji
Area: 699 sq km
Population: 100 000
Capital: Nuku'alofa
Economy: Mainly agriculture
Currency: Pa'anga

Trinidad and Tobago (Republic of Trinidad and Tobago)
In the Caribbean Sea, north of Venezuela
Area: 5 000 sq km
Population: 1 240 000
Capital: Port-of-Spain
Economy: Mainly oil production and refining
Currency: Dollar

Tunisia (Republic of Tunisia)
In Africa, bordered by Libya and Algeria (independence 1956)
Area: 164 000 sq km
Population: 7 200 000
Capital: Tunis
Economy: Mainly agriculture; some mining
Currency: Dinar

Turkey (Republic of Turkey)
In Europe, bordered by Soviet Union, Iran, Iraq, Syria, Greece and Bulgaria
Area: 781 000 sq km
Population: 48 450 000
Capital: Ankara
Economy: Mainly agriculture and industry
Currency: Lira

Tuvalu
In Pacific Ocean, north east of Australia
Area: 26 sq km
Population: 8 000
Capital: Funafuti
Economy: Mainly agriculture
Currency: Australian dollar

Uganda (Republic of Uganda)
In Africa, bordered by Zaïre, Sudan, Kenya, Tanzania and Rwanda (independence 1962)
Area: 236 000 sq km
Population: 15 200 000
Capital: Kampala
Economy: Mainly agriculture; some mining
Currency: New shilling

United Arab Emirates
In Asia, bordered by Qatar, Oman and Saudi Arabia
Area: 84 000 sq km
Population: 1 500 000
Capital: Abu Dhabi
Economy: Mainly oil production and refining
Currency: Dirham

United Kingdom (United Kingdom of Great Britain and Northern Ireland)
In Europe, north of France and bordered by Ireland
Area: 244 000 sq km
Population: 56 050 000
Capital: London
Economy: Mainly commerce and manufacturing; some agriculture
Currency: Pound sterling

United States of America
In North America, bordered by Canada and Mexico
Area: 9 363 000 sq km
Population: 233 500 000
Capital: Washington DC
Economy: Mainly commerce and manufacturing; some agriculture
Currency: Dollar

Uruguay (The Eastern Republic of Uruguay)
In South America, bordered by Brazil and Argentina
Area: 178 000 sq km
Population: 2 990 000
Capital: Montevideo
Economy: Mainly agriculture
Currency: Peso

Vanuatu (Republic of Vanuatu)
In Pacific Ocean, north east of Australia
Area: 15 000 sq km
Population: 130 000
Capital: Port-Vila
Economy: Mainly agriculture and tourism
Currency: Vatu

Vatican City (State of the Vatican City)
Headquarters of Roman Catholic Church, in Rome, Italy
Area: 0,44 sq km
Population: 1 000
Economy: All economic activity is connected with the Church
Currency: Lira

Venezuela (Republic of Venezuela)
In South America, bordered by Colombia, Brazil and Guyana
Area: 912 000 sq km
Population: 15 210 000
Capital: Caracas
Economy: Mainly agriculture and oil production
Currency: Bolivar

Vietnam (Socialist Republic of Vietnam)
In Asia, bordered by China, Laos and Kampuchea
Area: 333 000 sq km
Population: 58 000 000
Capital: Hanoi
Economy: Mainly agriculture
Currency: Dong

Western Samoa (Independent State of Western Samoa)
In Pacific Ocean, north east of New Zealand
Area: 3 000 sq km
Population: 170 000
Capital: Apia
Economy: Mainly agriculture
Currency: Tala

South Yemen (Aden) (People's Democratic Republic of Yemen)
In Asia, bordered by Saudi Arabia, Oman and Yemen (Sana)
Area: 336 000 sq km
Population: 2 000 000
Capital: Aden
Economy: Mainly shipping and oil refining
Currency: Dinar

NorthYemen (Sana) (The Yemen Arab Republic)
In Asia, bordered by Saudi Arabia and Yemen (Aden)
Area: 195 000 sq km
Population: 6 280 000
Capital: Sana
Economy: Mainly agriculture; some industry
Currency: Rial

Yugoslavia (Socialist Federal Republic of Yugoslavia)
In Europe, bordered by Italy, Austria, Hungary, Romania, Bulgaria, Greece and Albania
Area: 256 000 sq km
Population: 23 200 000

Capital: Belgrade
Economy: Mainly manufacturing and mining; some agriculture
Currency: Dinar

Zaïre (Republic of Zaïre)
In Africa, bordered by Congo, Central Africa Republic, Sudan, Uganda, Rwanda, Burundi, Tanzania, Angola and Zambia (independence 1960)
Area: 2 345 000 sq km
Population: 30 850 000
Capital: Kinshasa
Economy: Mainly mining; some agriculture
Currency: Zaïre

Zambia (Republic of Zambia; formerly Northern Rhodesia)
In Africa, bordered by Zaïre, Tanzania, Malawi, Mozambique, Zimbabwe, Botswana, Namibia and Angola (independence 1964)
Area: 753 000 sq km
Population: 6 300 000
Capital: Lusaka
Economy: Mainly mining; some agriculture and industry
Currency: Kwacha

Zimbabwe (see Part One: Facts about Zimbabwe)

PART FOUR

English Language

INTRODUCTION

You can use this section in the following ways:

- as a checklist for the general use of English;
- as a means of testing each other on the use of English;
- to revise what you have already covered in English language classes;
- to brush up on your writing skills.

The section can only cover some general areas of English. You should consult a good dictionary or a grammar book to check finer details if you find you need more information.

STRUCTURES AND FUNCTIONS

Languages are made up of **structures** and **functions**. **Structures** are the forms of grammatical components of the language. We need to know how to use them to be able to speak and write effectively. There are many logical rule-like approaches we can follow. However, real English is used by real people so you should pay attention to how the language is being used around you by teachers, friends and family, and in newspapers, magazines and books. Language structures are important, but so too are what we call language **functions**. We use languages to communicate with one another. Language functions are the labels we can give to what we do with language beyond just the parts of a sentence. An example would be a **request** you could make to a friend to help you with something: *Tafirenyika, please help me carry the box. It's too heavy for me.*

I. STRUCTURES

1 Sentences

English word forms (nouns, verbs, adverbs, etc.) are arranged in sentences through which meaning is expressed. There are several different types of sentences.

(a) Types of sentences

Sentences can be—

(i)	positive statements:	*Your hair is beautiful.*
(ii)	negative statements:	*The date on the letter is wrong.*
(iii)	questions:	*Are you always late?*
(iv)	imperatives:	*Stop right there!*
(v)	exclamations:	*Wonderful!*

(b) Order in sentences

The word order of sentences is important. In English there are two main parts of the sentence. They are the noun phrase (NP) and the verb phrase (VP). The verb phrase can be lengthened, or extended, in a number of ways. The noun phrase can also be lengthened or extended.

(+ extension)	noun phrase	verb phrase	(+ extension)
	My head	hurts.	
	We	missed	the bus.
	Tafadzwa	is	very bright.
	The shop	is	over the street.
In 1980	Zimbabwe	became	independent.

(c) Main clauses and supporting clauses

(i) Sentences are made up of main clauses and supporting clauses.

(ii) A main clause can stand on its own as a sentence which has clear meaning:

It was a long way from Tafara to the centre of Harare.

(iii) Two main clauses can be joined together with **and** or **but**:

*The girl used the money for the bus **and** her sister had to walk to school.*

(iv) Supporting clauses (also called subordinate clauses) allow you to use a main clause and add information to it. A supporting clause does not usually makes sense on its own. There can be number of different supporting clauses: they can tell us why, when, where, how, how much, the reason, the way and the result of something in the main clause.

(d) Compound sentences and complex sentences

(i) Main clauses can be combined to form compound sentences:

*She said she would be there **and** she really was there.* (**conjunction**)
She said she would come; she wore a pink dress. (**semi-colon**)

(ii) Complex sentences are those that have a main clause and one or more supporting clauses:

She was disappointed	*when she heard*	*that he had missed the train.*
(main clause)	(supporting clause)	(supporting clause)

When the train arrived	*she ran up to a man*	*who was not her brother.*
(supporting clause)	(main clause)	(supporting clause)

(iii) There are also sentences which have two main clauses and two supporting clauses:

After O Level	*they wrote to the Polytechnic*	*and asked for entry forms*	*which they needed in order to register there.*
(supporting clause)	(main clause)	(main clause joined by **and**)	(supporting clause)

(e) Ordering sentences into paragraphs

(i) Sentences are organized into paragraphs. We can describe paragraphs as idea units. Each paragraph should state one key idea and then develop it in detail. A new paragraph, therefore, signals the start of a new point or the introduction of a different or new idea.

(ii) A paragraph will usually have a key or topic sentence at the beginning or the end of the paragraph. This sentence is used to organize the other points.

(iii) Sentences within a paragraph must flow. Ideas and points need to be connected. You should use clear linking words and pronouns where appropriate. Each paragraph should also connect with the ones that go before it.

(iv) In addition to the main part of an essay, a good essay should have an introductory paragraph and a paragraph which pull together the material into a conclusion.

2 Verbs

Verbs are used in sentences to express action or states. They describe how things happen or how they appear, come into being or are destroyed. Verbs can have nouns or pronouns as their subjects. There are several important terms you need to know for this section. They are:

(a) Tense

Verbs have parts which do not change. These are called the base forms or **stems**: e.g. 'walk' remains unchanged in all the different tenses of the verb 'to walk'. English adds different endings to the stem of the verb. These different endings are called **markers**. Their purpose is to indicate the time which the verb is telling us about. The different times that verbs can show are called **tenses**. English verbs cover three broad time areas: present, past and future. Within each of these three areas there are a number of different expressions of time.

(b) Infinitive: to consider

The infinitive form of the verb can be used in the following ways—

(i) as subject: **To draw** well is difficult.

(ii) after verb: I want **to go** to the Victoria Falls. It's starting **to get** cold.

(iii) verb + object + infinitive: She persuaded me **to go** with them.

(iv) after adjective: I was amazed **to hear** the outcome of the inquiry

(v) verb + question word + infinitive: Can you tell me where **to pay?**

(c) Imperative: Get out!

We use the imperative to—

(i) command: **Take** that book to the library immediately.

(ii) instruct: **Mix** one spoon of flour with half a cup of water.

(iii) offer: Please, **take** mine, I don't need them.

(iv) warn: **Do** be careful on the roads this Easter.

- We also use the form 'Let's' when making suggestions:

   Let's go swimming.

(d) Active and passive

(i) Active verbs describe what people or things **do**:

   She **knitted** the jersey and **gave** it to her friend.

(ii) We use passive verbs to describe what **happens** to people or things: *The jersey* **was knitted** *by Jesrina.*
The passive allows us to say by whom/what the action was done at the end of the sentence.

(iii) Forms of passive:

Tense	Example
simple present	*Swahili is taught here.*
present continuous	*Your watch is being repaired now.*
simple past	*You were asked to do this by today.*
past progressive	*We thought we were being observed.*
present perfect	*I have been asked to attend the class.*
past perfect	*He had been represented by a weak lawyer.*
future	*You will know him when you see him.*
future perfect	*The well will have been dug before the rains.*
going to	*When is a cheap car going to be produced?*

(e) Main verb

The main verb occurs in what is called the verb phrase (VP). The verb phrase is the part of the sentence which tells us what is happening. (NP) stands for noun phrase. The noun phrase includes the subject.

NP	VP	NP
The man	*sighed.*	
The woman	*laughed*	*at her friend.*
They	*were becoming poorer.*	

(f) Types of verbs

(i) Transitive verbs: are followed by nouns
The boy **ate** *the cake.*

(ii) Intransitive verbs: are not followed directly by a noun
The train **stopped**.

(iii) Verbs + adjective: used to link the subject with the rest of the sentence and are followed by nouns or adjectives
The man **looked** *strange.*

(iv) The verb 'be': *They* **are** *famous.*

(g) Irregular verbs

English has many irregular verbs. They can be categorized as:

(i) The same infinitive, past tense and past participle

hurt	*hurt*	*hurt*
(infinitive)	*(past tense)*	*(past participle)*

(ii) Only past tense and past participle are the same

sleep	*slept*	*slept*
(infinitive)	*(past tense)*	*(past participle)*

(iii) infinitive, past tense and past participle are all different

take	*took*	*taken*
(infinitive)	*(past tense)*	*(past participle)*

• See page 103 for explanation about participles

(h) TENSES

(1) PRESENT TENSE

Simple present: **I walk**

This tense is used with—

(i) things that happen again and again: *We walk to school every day.*

(ii) for things that are happening for a limited period, not just for a moment: *He learns Ndebele at the local school.*

(iii) facts that remain the same over time: *I am tall.*

(iv) feelings: *I love . . . I want.*

(v) thoughts: *I think . . . I understand.*

(vi) verbs of reporting: *He says . . .*

(vii) verbs of possession: *I have . . .*

(viii) telling a story:

> *The man **runs** across the street. He **sees** the fire. He **searches** for a phone.*

> It can be used to relate something that is happening in the present:
> *Dynamos **have** the ball. Moyo **passes** it to Makoni.*

Present continuous: **He is talking.**

This tense is used with—

> things happening at the moment:
> *Please be quiet. **I am listening** to the speech.*

(2) PAST TENSE

Simple past: **It crawled** into the hole. **They went** to Masvingo.

This tense is used to—

(i) describe things that happened at a time which has now passed:
*Last month he **visited** her in Hwange.*

(ii) tell a story:
*It all **happened** a long time ago when we went to Masvingo. We **travelled** by bus.*

Present perfect: **I have** eaten/she **has** eaten/ they **have** eaten

This tense is used to—

(i) describe the present result of a past action:
*Careful! I **have worked** on it all day.*

(ii) describe something that happened a short time ago:
*He **has** just **gone out.***

(iii) describe something we are expecting someone to do:
*Have you **paid** the licence yet?*

(iv) mention something that has happened but has not stopped happening:
*He **has been waiting** at Gwanda since early this morning.*

(v) mention something that began in the past and has stayed the same
*It **has been** at the growth point for six months now.*

Past perfect: After we **had walked** to town, we ate lunch.

This tense is used to—

> mention the thing that happened first when we are talking about

things that happened in the past:
*After we **had** passed O Level, we decided to form a co-op.*

Past continuous: I was **eating** rice when I bit into a stone.
This tense is used to—
  (i) describe things that happened at a time in the past:
      *I was **waiting** for the bus for two hours yesterday!*
 (ii) to describe a situation where something was happening for some
      time and was interrupted by something which happened for a
      shorter time:
      *I was **cooking** sadza when there was a knock at the door.*
(iii) express a longer action that is interrupted:
      *When her sister arrived, I was still **plaiting** Tsitsi's hair.*
 (iv) describe two actions that happened at the same time:
      *While the bus driver was **checking** the tyres, people were **saying**
          goodbye to their relatives.*
  (v) tell a story:
      *It was a very dull day. The rain was **falling** ...*
• Some verbs are used in the continuous form: e.g. want, know

Present perfect continuous: I **have been** living in Mali for two years.
This tense is used to—
  (i) show something which began in the past and has gone on for some
      time:
      *Maiti has **been coming** top of the class since 1988.*
 (ii) describe something which is still going on:
      *You have **been talking** for a long time. Let Jasper have a turn
          now.*
(iii) describe something that finished a short time ago:
      *I have **been weeding** the field, and now I need a drink of water.*

Past perfect continuous: We **had been** studying there for two years.
This tense is used to—
      describe something that went on up to a point in the past:
      *Esnut was tired because she **had been plaiting** Jane's hair all
          morning.*

Used to: Our parents **used to** read us stories.
This is used to—
      describe something that happened in the past but no longer
      happens:
      *We **used to be** good friends before I left to live in Gweru.*

(3) FUTURE TENSE
To express things or actions in the future we can use future forms and
present tense forms.

Present continuous: We **are** travelling to Buhera for Christmas.
This tense is used to—
      say something is happening in the future – usually planned, and
      details are often given:
      *I am **holding** a party next Saturday.*

Going to: He **is going to** be a father.

We use going to when—
  (i) mentioning plans or intentions:
      *Memory telephoned. She's **going to** call again.*
  (ii) something will happen:
      *It's **going to** rain by the look of it.*

Future shall/will: I/she **will** beat you at cards.

Will and shall are used to—
  (i) show something is not yet decided:
      *Who do you think **will** win the history prize this year?*
  (ii) show something is definitely decided:
      *It **will** be impossible for me to buy the radio. I have $110 and it costs $155.*

• Try to use **shall** for offers – it is more polite:
      ***Shall** I help you with that?*
      Only use **shall** in the first person:
      *I **shall** . . .* but NOT *He shall*. Instead, say – *he will . . .*
      Use **will** for promises and threats:
      *I **will** be there on time. I **will** stop talking to you if you do that again.*

Simple present with future meaning: I will call you when I **come** to town.

This tense is used to—
  (i) talk about the future:
      *The term **begins** on 17 January.*
  (ii) express the future after conjunctions:
      *I will call you when I **land** at the airport.*

Present continuous with future meaning: We **are** driving to Chibi tomorrow.

The present continuous can express future meaning, and is used to—
  talk about plans or times in the future:
      *Our lift **is leaving** at 7 a.m.*

Future perfect: I **will have** finished.

This tense is used to—
  say something will have been done by a set time:
      *I **will have** been a grandmother for three years at Easter.*
      *I **will have** finished the job by Wednesday.*

Future continuous: I **will be** visiting.

This tense can be used to—
  describe something which will happen at some time in the future:
      *This time next week I **will be staying** in Mutare.*

Be to:

This is used to—
  express formal arrangements and is used in written English:
      *The President **is to** visit Angola in March.*

Be about to: I am about to leave.

This is used to—

>describe something which is going to happen in the very near future:
>
>*I am about to phone her – hold on.*

(i) Auxiliary verbs: be, have, do

Auxiliary verbs are used to—

(i) add to the main verb to create tenses:
>*I am sending you a cheque for $50. I have sent you a cheque.*

(ii) to give people advice or instructions:
>*Come on. Don't be shy.*

(iii) for emphasis:
>*Do be careful, won't you? The roads are wet.*

(iv) to replace verbs already mentioned:
>*He likes Coke and so do I.*

(j) Modal verbs: can, could, may, might, must, will, would, should, ought, dare and need.

Modal verbs are very important for effective communication in English. They are a difficult area of the language and you should take particular care to check whether you have used them appropriately and correctly.

Modal verbs are used to—

(i) say if something is allowed: can, may, be allowed to:
>*People **can/may/are allowed to** buy alcohol in Zimbabwe when they are 18 years old.*

(ii) ask permission: can, may, be allowed to:
>*Can you lend me your pen?*
>*May I use your phone?*

• **May** is a more formal expression than **can.**

(iii) show whether someone is able to do something: can, could, be able to:
>*He **can** swim, but I can't. He **could** walk before my other children.*
>*They **were able to** cross the flooded river.*

(iv) express necessity: must, have to:
>*I **must** be in Bulawayo by five for a meeting.*
>*Help, I **have to** get to the clinic. I think I've broken my arm.*

(v) show there is no necessity: need not, must not:
>*You **need not** come to the discussion tomorrow.*
>*You **must not** worry about your results.*

(vi) show something is not allowed: must not:
>*You **must not** drive more than 60 kph in built up areas.*

(vii) say what the right thing is to do: ought to, should:
>*You **ought to** wear blue more often. It suits you.*
>*He **should** see a doctor – he has a very high temperature.*

(viii) express possibility: may, might:
>*The book **may** be on that shelf, or the one above it.*
>*They said they **might** come tomorrow.*

(ix) express possibility: could
could is also used to express possibility but it is less certain than
may or might:
*The book **could** be on the shelf.*
could is used to suggest possibility in the future:
*We **could** meet at six if that's OK with you?*

(x) express something we are imagining – would:
*It **would** be wonderful if we could stay home tomorrow.*

(xi) express certainty: will, must:
*She finished first so she **will** get the prize.*
*The trousers have shrunk. You **must** have washed them in very
hot water.*

(xii) express a challenge or show we are afraid to do something: dare
*I **dare** you to climb that tall tree before the teacher arrives.*
*I **dare** not ask my father for money.*

- Modal verbs are also used with be + -ing forms:
*Tendai may **be** wear**ing** the brightest dress, but yours is smarter.*

- Modal verbs are also used with have + -ed forms:
*We should **have** been inform**ed** that the lecture was cancelled.*

3 Participles

The participle is a form that can be added to the verb stem. Although
participles are usually called present (-ing) and past (-ed), both these
endings can be used to describe actions in the past, present and future:

(i) *Look at that man dri**ving** on the wrong side of the road.* (present)
(ii) *She was loo**king** well when I saw her.* (past)
(iii) *This time next week I'll be travel**ling** to Chipinge.* (future)
(iv) *You are want**ed** by the secretary.* (present)
(v) *He was detain**ed** in 1972.* (past)
(vi) *The matter is going to be contest**ed** in court next week.* (future)

- Participles can also be used as adjectives:
*You look completely exhaust**ed**.* (present)
*The exhibition was disappoint**ing**.* (past)

4 Negatives

(a) Negative statements

(i) **Not** can be used with **be** or **have**, modal verbs:
*I am **not** going with you to Bulawayo. I have **not** found my suit-
case. In any case you can't wait for me till after work and if you do
you might **not** get there in time. I don't want you to wait for me.*

(ii) **No, no-one, nobody, nothing, nowhere, none, either, nor,
never** are used in negative statements:
*There was **no** petrol in the car. **Nobody** drove down the road. We
had **neither** water **nor** food. There was **nothing** we could do but
wait. I had **never** been so thirsty and there was **nowhere** I could
think I'd rather be than at home with a bottle of water!*

(b) Negative questions

These are used to—
  (i) ask for information: *Why haven't they got their exam results?*
  (ii) suggest: *Why don't you come along with us?*
  (iii) to show surprise: *Haven't you seen it yet?*
  (iv) to ask if someone agrees: *Didn't I meet you with Mercy yesterday?*

5 Reported speech

Reported speech puts what was actually said (direct speech) into a different form:

  original   *Tererai said, "I want to be a banker."*
  reported speech   *Tererai said that he wanted to be a banker.*

• Note that tenses change when using reported speech:
  Can you help me with this box? becomes *She asked him if he could help her with the box.*

• Note that we do not use question marks in reported speech.

We can also use reported speech in the following ways:
  (i) *He asked me if I had ever been to Kariba.*
  (ii) *The doctor asked me what I had eaten.*
  (iii) *The doctor advised me to drink lots of water with the tablets.*
  (iv) *She knew what they had planned.* (or with other verbs describing thoughts or beliefs.)
  (v) *Sipiwe said she didn't like the fabric.*
  (vi) *They asked how to find their way to Mbare.*
    but not . . . *they asked how did they find their way to Mbare.*
  (vii) *Jennifer asked us to turn down the radio.*

6 Nouns

  (i) Nouns have traditionally been said to be the name of a person, place or thing. This can be confusing because some words have the same form but can be nouns and verbs: e.g. smell. We need to look at the **place of nouns in sentences** and ask what **function** they perform.

  (ii) A noun can be the **subject** of a sentence. It can also be the **object** of a sentence:

subject		*object*
The woman	drove	the bus.
(noun phrase)	(verb phrase)	(noun phrase)

Nouns can be classified as:

common nouns	**proper nouns**
horse, truck	Zambia, Zaire
abstract nouns	**concrete nouns**
desire	bricks
countable nouns	**uncountable nouns**
a kitten/two kittens	honey/jars of honey
one cent/ten cents	money/wads of money
some visitors	lightning/vivid lightning in the sky

In addition there are some nouns – sometimes called collective nouns –
which have very particular words that we use to indicate that there is
a number or quantity of them/it.

birds	flock of birds
bees	swarm of bees
cattle	herd of cattle
cotton	bale of cotton
directors	board of directors
lions	pride of lions
monkeys	troop of monkeys
oxen	team of oxen
paper	ream of paper

measurement nouns	**type nouns**
a cup of tea	a make of radio

Plurals of nouns

(a) Regular plurals of nouns

my book   our books   an axe   two axes

(b) Irregular plurals of nouns

a tomato	a kilo of tomatoes	a foot	ten feet
a lorry	many lorries	her goose	several geese
a loaf	two loaves	a mouse	many mice
her child	their children	a woman	ten women
a sheep	several sheep	a person	some people

Nouns: youth and age

There are nouns which have different terms for young or offspring and
for adults of the species. A few examples are listed here:

offspring/young	*adult/old*
cub	bear
kitten	cat
cockerel	cock
calf (male) heifer (female)	cow
puppy	dog
duckling	duck
eaglet	eagle
chick	fowl
tadpole	frog
kid	goat
gosling	goose
pullet	hen
larva	insect
piglet	pig
lamb	sheep

Nouns: male and female

There are nouns which are used to refer to specific male and female
groups.

Some examples are listed below:

male	female	group
bachelor	spinster	(unmarried person)
buck	doe	(antelope)
colt	filly	(horse)
gander	goose	(geese)
monk	nun	(religious orders)
ram	ewe	(livestock)
uncle	aunt	(family relations)

N.B. See also 'sexist terms' in the section on vocabulary below.

7 Pronouns

Pronouns can be used to stand in for a noun which has already been mentioned. There are a number of different types of pronouns:

(a) **Personal pronouns**: I, you, he, she, it, me, him, her, we, they, us, them.

These are used to—

   (i) refer back to the mentioned subject: *And Precious? Is she still angry?*

   (ii) refer to the person speaking/present: *Yes, I agree with you.*

(b) **Possessive pronouns**: mine, yours, his, hers, its, ours, theirs

These are used to—

   indicate ownership: *Yes, the house in Kuwadzana is his.*

(c) **Reflexive pronouns**: myself, ourselves, yourself, yourselves, him self, herself, itself, themselves

These are used to—

   (i) refer back to the subject already mentioned:
      John himself was a prophet. He had visionary powers.

   (ii) emphasize the subject: *She herself asked you to do this.*

(d) **Relative pronouns**: that, which, who, whom, whose

These are used to—

   refer back to the noun already mentioned in the sentence:
   Here is the girl who helped me find my watch.

(e) **Demonstrative pronouns**: this, that, these, those

These are used to—

   (i) point out something nearby: *These tomatoes look over-ripe.*

   (ii) point out something further off: *I like those over there.*

(f) **Indefinite pronouns**: either, neither, each, both, all, some, many, few, something, someone, somebody, anything, anybody, anyone, nothing, nobody, no-one, one, none.

These are used to—

   refer to nouns where the amount or quantity is not specific:
   Anyone can come in and buy anything they like.

(g) Impersonal pronouns: one, you, they
These are used to—
> leave the subject unnamed or refer to people in general:
> *You never know what people think.*
> *It is generally believed that smoking causes lung cancer.*

(h) Interrogative pronouns: who, what, which, whose
These are used to—
> ask questions: ***Which** drink would you like?*

8 Quantifiers

As their name suggests, quantifiers express quantity. Here are some examples:
  (i) **each** is used to talk about one from a small group:
  > *One girl from **each** class will represent the school.*
 (ii) **any** is used to refer to one from a large group:
  > *How will we find them. They could have taken **any** road on the map.*
(iii) **every** is used to refer to an unnamed group:
  > ***Every** writer needs to eat and sleep.*

Other quantifiers are: many, much, a lot, a few, a little, more, most, fewer, fewest, less, least, some, more, other, another, enough, plenty of, all, most, both, either, neither, no, none.

9 Articles

These take the form: a/an/the
They are used to—
  (i) refer to one member of a group: *She is **a** generous donor.*
 (ii) describe things belonging to a group/type: *Zanzibar is **an** island.*
(iii) refer to something known: ***The** one I already mentioned*
(iv) refer to something already mentioned:
  > *He has a blue suit and a black suit. **The** black one is smarter.*
 (v) when the situation indicates what is meant:
  > *I'll see you in **the** office later.*

10 Adjectives

Adjectives are used—
  (i) to tell us more about nouns or pronouns;
 (ii) in the same form, usually for singular and plural:
  > *a hungry boy, hungry children.*
(iii) usually before the noun: *a **beautiful** sculpture;*
  but with 'be' it can come after the noun:
  > *That sculpture is magnificent.*

Adjectives have **comparative** and **superlative** forms:

Comparative adjectives are used to compare one thing with another or others: *John was **shorter** than Eunice.*
• Note the use of **than.**

- Note also that you cannot use **very** with comparatives. We use **much** or **far** instead.

    *The river was **much** deeper than we expected.*
    We also use ***very much**, any, rather, a lot, a little.*

Superlative adjectives are used to compare one thing with a whole group: *Eunice was the **tallest** person in the room.*

- Note the use of **the.**
- Note also that you can use the superlative without a noun:

    *Which do you think is **prettiest?***

Comparison of regular adjectives:

*She is a **clever** person.*	STANDARD
*It is an **acceptable** price.*	
*She is **cleverer** than Alexander.*	COMPARATIVE
*This is **more acceptable than** the other.*	
*She is **the cleverest** person I know.*	SUPERLATIVE
*It is **the most acceptable** teapot.*	

Comparison of irregular adjectives:

*She is **good** at his job.*	STANDARD
*He is **better** looking without his hat on.*	COMPARATIVE
*He is the **best** guitarist in the city.*	SUPERLATIVE

Comparative adjectives are also used—
  (i) to compare similar or dissimilar things:
     *The bus is **as** expensive **as** the emergency taxi.*
     *The tyre was not **as** new **as** he thought it was.*
 (ii) with 'and': *The hole was growing **deeper** and **deeper**.*
(iii) with 'the': ***The shorter** my hair, **the easier** it is to comb.*

- Note that nearest = closest, latest = newest

Adjectives are also used to—
  (i) describe colours and are used like nouns: *He hates **pink**.*
 (ii) refer to people from different countries: *The proprietor is **Zambian**.*

11 Adverbs

Adverbs are used to—
  (i) describe **how** something happens: e.g. angrily, fast:
     *The river flowed **swiftly**.*
 (ii) say **how often** something happens: e.g. sometimes, never,
     occasionally: *We **usually** catch the 6.30 bus.*
(iii) relate **where** or **when** something happens: e.g. down, later:
     *We could meet them **later**.*
 (iv) make the meaning of an adjective or verb either stronger or
     weaker: *I **nearly** fell into the mud.*
  (v) to reveal the speaker's attitude: ***Fortunately**, I like the fellow.*

Adverbs take different forms:
  (i) adjective + **-ly** e.g. *swiftly* (but note: some adjectives keep the
     same form, e.g. an *elderly* woman).

(ii) many adverbs have the same form as adjectives: e.g. late;

(iii) some adverbs do not follow a set form: e.g. fast, perhaps, so, away;

(iv) we can also use additional words which perform the function of an adverb: *in an aloof* **manner** / *in a most unfriendly* **way**.

Position of adverbs:

(i) front: **Occasionally** *I smoke a pipe.*

(ii) middle: *The painting is* **definitely** *an original.*

(iii) end: *He opened the book* **carefully**.

Comparison of regular adverbs:

(i) *He drove the car* **slowly**.	STANDARD
(ii) *He began to drive* **more slowly**.	COMPARATIVE
(iii) *You drive* **most slowly** *in the rain.*	SUPERLATIVE

Comparison of irregular adverbs:

(i) *He drove the bus* **badly**.	STANDARD
(ii) *He drove* **worse** *than usual.*	COMPARATIVE
(iii) *He was the* **worst** *driver on the road*	SUPERLATIVE

Comparisons are worded as follows:

(i) **The more** *you read,* **the better** *your vocabulary.*

(ii) *You can easily run* **as fast as** *she can.*

(iii) *The music became* **faster and faster**.

Adverbial phrases

The function of adverbs is also carried out in other ways:

(i) prepositional phrases: *He baked the cake* **expertly** (adverb) **with experience** (prepositional phrase);

(ii) infinitive: *She dressed* **quickly** (adverb) **to get** *to work early.* (verb phrase).

(iii) + -ing: *Drumming her fingers, she waited for the water to boil.* (- ing form);

(iv) + - ed: *Encouraged by the crowd, the team won the match.* (- ed form).

12 Prepositions

Prepositions are used to—

(i) indicate a connection with a noun: *The cow was* **in** *the pen.*

(ii) modify nouns: *The cow* **in the pen** *was the wrong one.* (prepositional phrase)

(iii) modify verbs: *They walked* **up and down** *the stairs at least ten times a day.*

(iv) help form idiomatic expressions: *In the end he* **came over** *to our side.*

Prepositions are used to tell us about the place where something happens. They can indicate—

(i) direction and movement:
The boy sprinted **across** *the field.*
She walked **down** *to the river.*

(ii) the position of objects in relation to other objects:
*She placed her purse **inside** her handbag.*
*The building was **between** third and fourth streets.*

(iii) types of places:
*The baby crawled **into** the room.*
*Ruvimbo's father walked **through** the room without noticing her.*
*They met **at** the junction of Samora Machel Avenue and Julius Nyerere Way.*
*She spread the blanket **across** the bed.*
*We ran **along** the river bank looking for a boat.*

Prepositions are usually small words but they are important words because they help relate parts of a sentence to other parts. The best way to learn how to use prepositions is to look out for them in books and magazines. You should note any prepositions with which you are unfamiliar and then try to use them accurately. When looking up prepositions in a dictionary remember to check how they are used in the examples that are provided.

13 Conjunctions

We use conjunctions to—
join two clauses: e.g. and, but, because, so, if, although:
*She was a powerful leader **and** an exceptionally generous person.*
*It rained yesterday **but** there wasn't enough rain to save the crops.*
*They stopped to give him a lift **because** he was her friend's brother.*
*The knife broke **so** he had to borrow one.*
*They would have paid on time **if** they had received the request.*
*He listened to the advice **although** he had no intention of using it.*

Some conjunctions are only used to link clauses: e.g. **and, but, so.**
Some conjunctions are used at the beginning of sentences:
If they had received the request, they would have paid on time.

• Note that a comma is used after the first clause when the sentence starts with a conjunction.

II. FUNCTIONS

The section above looks at particular language structures and the uses to which they can be put. All language exists to **do** something. Language is created and used by people who give it life. **Language functions** describe what we can do with language in components which are bigger than clauses and sometimes bigger than entire sentences.

1 Common language functions

Here are some commonly used language functions. The first example in each section is fairly formal. The second example is more friendly and informal. Note that it is not always necessary to use the specific function word in the sentence in order to perform the function e.g. see **inviting** below.

(i) asking—

"*I would be grateful if you could provide me with details of costs for the fittings.*"

"*Can we meet later, Peter?*"

(ii) thanking—

"*We would like to thank you for your generous donation to the library.*"

"*Thanks for your support. Your help really took the weight off my shoulders.*"

(iii) complaining—

"*I am afraid you must return this tin of peas to the factory. The tin is rusty and the peas are a peculiar colour.*"

"*Look, Jeff, you were late and I needed the key. You made things very difficult for me.*"

(iv) inviting—

"*The Chairperson of the Association would like to invite you to a small party after the conference.*"

"*Would you like to have lunch with me tomorrow?*"

(v) offering—

"*We would like to offer you a job in the factory from next week.*"

"*Please don't worry. You can have my ticket.*"

(vi) suggesting—

"*The Minister suggested that the meeting should continue the following day.*"

"*Perhaps we should leave later than we planned?*"

(vii) persuading—

"*It was a very good argument and one which should probably be included in the proposal.*"

"*Everyone knows what a good organizer you are. We could really do with your help.*"

(viii) describing—

"*The building will be impressive. It will have huge wooden doors that will open into a courtyard with a fountain in the middle.*"

"*They were a really cool and laid back couple.*"

(ix) evaluating—

"*The doctor said that there was little cause for concern.*"

"*I think your shirt is great.*"

2 Vocabulary

Vocabulary is the area in English which is probably changing faster than any other aspects of the language. Words are being created as technology develops and words are also introduced into the language from other languages.

Words can be broken up into parts. This helps us to make sense of them and to build our vocabulary by analysing the parts. However, words must be learned in relation to other words. The meaning of words depends on the **context** in which they occur. If you come across a new or unfamiliar word, do not stop and reach for the dictionary. Instead, read on. See if you can make sense of the word from the general feel of the paragraph or passage and from the words in the rest of the sentence. Meaning is something we build up when we read a passage.

(a) Word formation

(i) Parts of words: prefixes and suffixes.

Words can be broken up into roots, prefixes and suffixes. A **root** is the main part or stem of a word. Parts can be added to it. A **prefix** is placed in front of the root, and a **suffix** is placed after the root of the word. A root can exist on its own, or it can have a prefix, or a suffix or both. A root can also have more than one suffix.

Prefix	Root	Suffix/Suffixes	
	like	-ly	
pre-	view		
	thank	-ful	
dis-	agree	-ment	
	norm	-al	-ize

English has borrowed many of its prefixes and suffixes from Latin, Greek, and French. The variety of influences shows how languages change to include parts of other languages.

In the section below only a few prefixes and suffixes will be covered. You should consult a good dictionary for further help. There is often a section near the front of a dictionary which tells you what prefixes and suffixes mean and where they originated.

prefix	meaning	example	meaning
bi-	twice	bilateral	**bilateral** ageements involve exchanges between two groups
sub-	under below	**sub**conscious	the **subconscious** is the part of your mind below conscious thought which can still influence your actions

suffix	meaning	example	meaning
-arian	believer	authoritarian	A person who is **authoritarian** wants to control other people's thoughts, beliefs and actions
-ics	art	mathematics	**Mathematics** is the scientific activity study of numbers, quantities, science and shapes

(ii) Parts of words: markers

Parts of words can be altered to change the meaning from singular to plural, to show possession of something, or to show changes in the verb. Only the most common forms are shown below. Consult your dictionary for less common forms: e.g. 'stimulus stimuli'.

(a)	*singular nouns*	*plural nouns*	*marker*
	dog	dogs	-s
	shelf	shelves	-es
	baby	babies	-ies
	man	men	-e-
	foot	feet	-ee-

(b)	*possession (with nouns)*		*marker*
	Tendai	Tendai's	-'s
	girls	girls'	-s'
	women	women's	-'s

(c)	*verbs present*	*verbs past*	*marker*
	walk	walked	-ed
	dance	danced	-d
	try	tried	-ied

root	*past participle*	*marker*
rain	raining	-ing
rain	(has) rained	-ed
fall	(has) fallen	-en
grow	(has) grown	-n
build	(has) built	-t

root	*3rd person sing.*	*marker*
provide	provides	-s
try	tries	-ies
go	goes	-es

(iii) Parts of words: syllables

Words are made of syllables. Words can be made of one syllable, or more than one syllable. This applies to the different parts of the structure of English. Say words out loud to help you work out how many syllables they have. The table below provides some examples of the variety of syllables which can be used with different structures e.g. nouns or verbs:

	verb	noun	adjective	adverb
1	*grow*	*hand*	*good*	*now*
2	*grow-ing*	*hand-bag*	*care-ful*	*late-ly*
3	*en-ter-tain*	*ma-nag-er*	*com-fort-able*	*hap-pi-ly*
4	*de-moc-rat-ize*	*en-ter-tain-ment*	*dis-pas-sion-ate*	*un-cer-tain-ly*

(b) Meaning

The meaning of words is a little more complex than we usually think. Words can have one general meaning, several general meanings or a number of meanings, some general and some fairly specialist. Here are some examples:

'knobbly'	something which is knobbly has an uneven surface with lumps which stick out: e.g. a **knobbly** *old piece of wood.*
'prescribe'	(a) a doctor who **prescribes** medicine directs that you take particular medicine when you are ill;
	(b) if a duty is **prescribed,** then it must be done as if it were a rule.
'fair'	(a) can mean free from dishonesty or discrimination, unbiased – *he had a fair trial;*
	(b) can mean light in colouring – *she had very fair hair;*
	(c) can mean quite good – *the results of the English test were fair;*
	(d) can mean it is sunny or cloudless – *wonderfully fair weather;*
	(e) can mean thorough, difficult – *it was a fair battle to get on to the bus.*

(c) Variety in vocabulary

The vocabularies of languages change. This is particularly the case with English as it is used more widely than any other language in the world. Terms are borrowed from other languages. New terms are also created, particularly because English is used widely in education, science and technology. Often words are created out of other words. There are a number of ways in which words are introduced to the language.

(i) Vocabulary: compound words

Words can be formed by mixing parts of other words:

structure	*one word*	*hyphenated*
noun + noun	*handbook*	*box-office*
adj + noun	*hardware*	*left-wing*
noun + adj	*airtight*	*duty-free*
adverb + noun	*overdraft*	*up-market*
verb + adverb	*kickoff*	*print-out*
noun + verb	*manhunt*	*hand-made*
verb + noun	*playmate*	
verb + adj		*drip-dry*
adj + verb	*highflown*	*short-cut*
adverb + verb	*outfit*	*open-ended*
noun + adverb		*knock-out*
adverb + adj	*overripe*	
pronoun + noun		*he-man*

(ii) Vocabulary: coinages

These are new terms. They can be entirely new forms, but often they are formed by joining parts of two existing words:

coinage	*components*
computer	from verb 'to compute'
space shuttle	space + shuttle (to go back and forth in space)
news cast	news + broad (cast)
growth-point	growth + point

(iii) Vocabulary: borrowed terms

People and languages come into contact with one another and as a result many words have been introduced into English from other languages or countries:

> e.g. *focus* (Latin) *dingo* (Australian) *sofa* (Arabic) *sadza* (Shona)
> *kindergarten* (German) *apartheid* (South African)

Once the words have been absorbed into the language, they become a part of it and in written language we no longer distinguish them with underlining or italics. For example, we no longer think of 'guerilla' as being a Spanish word, or 'enterpreneur' as being a French one. A good dictionary will mention the origin of a word if it has been absorbed into the language from another language.

There are, however, some foreign words which we always recognize as such and when wording them they should be italicized and underlined. These are a few examples:

ad infinitum (Latin) – without end
aide-de-camp (French) – a military officer who assists superior
coup d'état (French) – illegal change of government, often by force
per capita (Latin) – of or for each person
subpoena (Latin) – official written order to appear in court

(iv) Vocabulary: specialist terms

Many disciplines use words in ways special to the disciplines. Sometimes this means a common word takes a special meaning ('market' in economics) and sometimes a specialist term exists in a special field ('carburettor' in motor mechanics). Check these terms with a dictionary and note them down when you come across them in your reading. Newspapers and magazines often have a variety of ordinary terms (in the general part of the paper) and specialist terms (in adverts, the classified section, in business and sports sections, etc.).

(d) Related words: Synonyms, Antonyms, Homonyms

Languages do not have words which have exactly the same or opposite meaning. After all, we have the variety of words that we do so that they can express the meaning we need them to express. All meaning comes from the context within which words are used. Words therefore cannot have the exact same or opposite meaning. However, there are instances where words can replace one another or express fairly clear opposites. Words can be said to have two broad types of meaning: meaning that **refers** to something concrete (*knife* = sharp cutting instrument with handle) and meaning that the word **suggests** (*red* = hot/angry/blood/socialist).

Many words have more than one meaning. They may have—
  (i) more than one structural form;
 (ii) general meaning only;
(iii) a number of different general meanings;
(iv) general meaning and a specialized meaning;
 (v) specialized meaning only;
(vi) one or a number of specialized meanings.

It is important that we remember that it is possible for one word to have a variety of meanings. This is particularly important when we are dealing with synonyms and antonyms. **Synonyms** are words that have similar meanings to other words. **Antonyms** are words that have opposite meanings to other words. Most dictionaries record whether words have synonyms or antonyms. The section below therefore includes only a few examples.

(i) Synonyms

Here are some examples of synonyms:

A **down-payment** is the payment of the part of a sum of money and is usually paid at the start of the purchasing: e.g. a down-payment of $10 000 on a house. Instead of the word down-payment we could use the word **deposit**.

The **character** of a person, people, or thing is made up of the qualities they have which go to make up personality or atmosphere. Instead of character we could say **nature**.

Remember when you are looking for words to replace or rephrase other words you should check that the replacement fits the sentence and that the meaning is not changed. Sometimes you may have to use more than one word to express the same meaning.

(ii) Antonyms

Antonyms are perhaps more difficult to work out, so a list of some antonyms is given below. Remember that a word can have more than one meaning and therefore more than one synonym or more than one antonym:

word	example	antonym
rough	The table has a very rough surface (uneven)	smooth (level = even)
	It is a very rough neighbourhood (tough)	smart (peaceful = unviolent)

Antonyms:

accept	reject	hot	cold
agreement	disagreement	initial	final
amateur	professional	join	separate
approve	condemn/reject	lead	follow
attack	defend	often	seldom
bravery	cowardice	permit	prohibit
broad	narrow	premature	overdue
cautious	reckless	proud	humble
cheap	expensive	rough	smart
dynamic	static	rough	smooth
eager	reluctant	sharp	blunt
familiar	strange	truth	falsehood
front	rear	whole	part
graceful	awkward	victory	defeat

(ii) Homonyms

There are also many words which sound very similar but which are spelt differently. These words are called homonyms.

altar	alter	
bear	bare	
caught	court	
council	counsel	
draft	draught	
ewe	you	
guessed	guest	
heard	herd	
least	leased	
peace	piece	
pray	prey	
queue	cue	
rain	reign	
sent	cent	scent
wear	ware	where
week	weak	
wholly	holy	

Note: some words have more than one homonym. Note also that homonyms often include words which function as structures: e.g. pray (verb), prey (noun). If you learned Ndebele or Shona as your first language, you may have some difficulty with homonyms. You may find that you hear and also perhaps pronounce some of the vowel sounds of English words similarly: e.g. *ship* and *sheep*. You should not worry about this, as long as you can make clear what you want to communicate.

(e) Shortened forms

Most languages shorten commonly used terms, particularly ones which are used regularly in formal writing. This can be done in a number of ways.

(i) Abbreviations

Abbreviations are fairly standardized and will often be included in entries in dictionaries. You will find that abbreviations are used in academic, technical and scientific areas: e.g. Herz = Hz. Note also the use of symbols as in Chemistry where, for example, Hg stands for mercury. Here are some examples of abbreviations:

AD	after Christ: from the Latin, *anno Domini,* meaning 'the year of the Lord'
ad.	advertisement
adj.	adjective
a.m.	before noon: from the Latin, *ante meridiem,* meaning 'before noon'
assn.	association
BC	before Christ
BSc.	Bachelor of Science
cert.	certificate

cf.	compare
deg.	degree
dept.	department
ed.	editor
eds	editors
e.g.	for example: from the Latin *exempli gratia*
etc.	and so on: from the Latin *et cetera*
Fr.	Father
geog.	geography
Hon.	Honourable
i.e.	that is: from the Latin *id est*
info	information
intro	introduction
Jan.	January
kg	kilogram
km	kilometre
Ltd	Limited
masc.	masculine
MD	Doctor of Medicine/Managing Director
mike	microphone
Mr	Mister
PM	Prime Minister
rep	representative
rpt	report
sing.	singular
St.	saint/street
tech.	technical
v.	versus/verb
viz.	namely

(ii) Shortened forms

We often shorten forms when the meaning of a word or term will not
be lost: e.g. rhinoceros = rhino, photograph = photo, aeroplane = plane.
We often shorten the word to half the number of its syllables.

(iii) Acronyms

An acronym is a string of letters which stand for the main words in the
title of an organization or group. Examples of these are: Non Aligned
Movement (NAM), Organization of African Unity (OAU). You should
look out for acronyms in newspapers, magazines and books and learn
them as you go along. Here are some examples of acronyms:

ANC	African National Congress
CDU	Curriculum Development Unit
PANA	Pan African News Agency
ZESA	Zimbabwe Electricity Supply Authority
ZDAWU	Zimbabwe Domestic and Allied Workers Union
ZTA	Zimbabwe Tobacco Association

3 Using a dictionary

Learners, and even expccerienced writers, of English need to refer to
dictionaries. You should try to obtain a dictionary of your own or refer
to one as often as possible.

Dictionaries provide alphabetical lists of words. Each listed word is called an entry. An entry for a word will tell you the possible meanings of the word. A good dictionary will use words in sentences to show their meaning. It will also tell you whether the word is used as a noun, verb, adjective etc. These structural labels are usually abbreviated and a list of the abbreviations is usually given at the front of the dictionary. Check this list because it can help you to understand how a word is being used.

When checking on the meaning of a word, remember to check it against the sentence in which the word appears. Ask yourself: does the meaning fit the sentence? If more than one meaning is given under the entry, check that you have selected the meaning which fits the sentence.

Remember that a dictionary is an aid to using words more effectively. The meaning of words depends on the other words in the sentence and the general point of view the writer is presenting.

A dictionary will also provide you with the full forms for most common abbreviations and acronyms. A good dictionary will usually tell you something about the origin of a borrowed word and, perhaps, also give information about synonyms and antonyms.

Many dictionaries also give guides to the pronunciation of words. Pronunciation tables and examples are usually placed at the beginning of the book before the entries for the letter 'a' begin.

4 Spelling

Accuracy in the use of structures is important, but so is the correct spelling of words. Words are made up of a number of parts. The smallest part is a unit of sound. Think of the two words *bad* and *bed*. They have two different meanings. This difference is shown by the change in the middle letters. Unfortunately, the spelling of English does not rely totally on the sound of words.

In addition to units of sound we have units of meaning. They have already been included in every page of this book. For example, we change the present tense of the verb 'dance' to the past tense form 'danced' by adding 'ed'.

We have already seen that words have stems or roots. It is important that we can identify these roots because they can help us work out meaning: e.g. govern = root = verb government = root + suffix (ment) = noun.

There are many words which are difficult to spell. This might be because they—

(i) do not look like what they sound like. You will have to learn and check these as you go along: e.g. 'those', where we pronounce the 's' more like a 'z'. In other cases, you might be influenced by the rules of sounds which usually go together in your first language: e.g. Shona speakers often spell *ship* and *sheep* the same way because they sound the same to them.

(ii) there are also words which have come into the language and have kept their original spelling. Very often these words are difficult to spell because they have parts which we do not pronounce: in 'technique' the 'que' is pronounced as one sound 'k'.

Here are a few more of the sorts of words to watch out for:

acquire	beautiful	conscious	government
parallel	receipt	scent	schedule

(iii) they are long words and have many syllables: e.g. apologetically.

Some spelling tips

Here are some tips for spelling. They will help to guide you, but you should be trying to spell accurately by reading as much as you can. You should note down new words which you find difficult to pronounce and spell. Write down the whole sentences in which they occur. Check the meanings of these words in a dictionary. Perhaps you and a friend could test one another on the spelling and meaning of these words:

(i) When a suffix begins with a vowel, leave out the 'e'
   tide + -al = tidal

(ii) When a suffix begins with a consonant, keep the 'e'
   polite + -ness = politeness

(iii) When a suffix begins with a vowel:
   (a) double the last consonant with monosyllables
      clap + -ing = clapping
   (b) if the last syllable is stressed, double the last consonant
      expel + -ed = expelled
   (c) if the last consonant follows a vowel, double the consonant
      prefer + -ed = preferred

(iv) final 'y' becomes 'i' except when suffix is 'ing'
   rely + -iance = reliance   rely + -ing = relying

(v) if the sound is 'ee', after 'c' write 'ei' and not 'ie': *receipt*

(vi) **gh** = sounds like 'f' in *laugh*

(vii) **gh** = sounds like 'f' in *enough*

(viii) **gh** = is silent in *taught*

(ix) **gh** = is silent in *sought*

5 Words in context

The variety of uses of words and expressions.

We have mentioned that words can have a number of meanings. Words can also be used in a variety of situations and for different reasons. We might need to communicate with a range of people and on a number of different topics. It is important that you think about these differences. You need to be able to choose your words to suit the different occasions and audiences. For example, you might call one of your friends a 'guy' when talking with other school friends, but you could not call him this if you had to talk to your head teacher, could you?

(a) Written and spoken English: formal and colloquial

Some words and expressions are more **formal**, polite and respectful than others. Then there are expressions which are more conversational and informal. We call these words and expressions **colloquial**. Formal and **informal** words can be used in both spoken and written English. A person can—

- make a formal speech to open a new school, before a large crowd of important people;
- speak casually with friends about what happened after school;
- write a formal essay as part of academic study, to be read by a teacher or examiner;
- write a very chatty and informal letter to a close friend.

Each time you look up a word in a dictionary you should look to see how it has been used in examples and whether the word is described as formal or informal, general or specialized in meaning.

(b) Circumlocution

Do not try to write or speak your way into what you want to communicate. Say what you have to say in short sentences with vocabulary that makes your points clearly. Do not try to impress your listener or reader with long and complicated words or sentences.

(c) Tautology

Avoid saying the same thing twice in the same sentence by using words that have the same or similar meaning. *In my opinion* NOT *in my own opinion:*

> *The house was painted beige* NOT *The house was painted a beige colour.*

(d) Sexist terms

Something or someone 'sexist' is based on the idea that one sex, usually the female sex, is deficient, inferior or less capable than the other sex. This usually suggests that certain jobs should be kept for one sex and not the other. The term 'sexist' is used by people, usually women, who refer to others who put women down (intentionally and unintentionally or thoughtlessly) and portray them as less valuable than men. Many societies now recognize that men and women are of equal emotional and mental strength. They should therefore have access to the same jobs at the same pay. This recognition has meant that words in the language have been adapted to show equality instead of difference. We might well ask why should there be two words for unmarried people? *The Herald* no longer advertises for 'Foremen' but now for 'Forepersons'.

Some tips for avoiding sexist use of language:

- Use 'they' instead of 'he' whenever possible – the tendency has always been for people to use 'he' when they mean both men and women;
- Use people/person instead of 'men' or 'man' meaning both men and women.

6 Idiomatic expressions

Words can have **literal** and **figurative** meaning. **Literal** meaning is the most basic meaning of a word. When we say something has

figurative meaning we are saying that the meaning is imaginative and abstract. In other words, the meaning is not the general meaning but may be associated with other things connected with the word.

The **idiomatic** use of language is **figurative**. An idiom is a group of words which has meaning because of their being grouped together. This meaning is different to that of the meaning of each of the individual words in the group of words. An idiom allows us to say something fairly detailed in a few words. It also allows us to say something indirectly – we do not need to say exactly what we want to say, instead we can suggest a connection and make a point without being too obvious.

Idiomatic expressions include: **proverbs, similes,** and **metaphors**.

(a) A **proverb** is a short sentence. It presents a truth about life and often advises you how to face it or deal with it. People often quote whole proverbs. An example of a proverb is *A stitch in time saves nine*. This means that if you act or do something early enough, you will save yourself a great deal of time and energy later. If you were looking up the meaning of this in a dictionary you would first look up the word 'stitch' and then the word 'time'. You would probably find the idiomatic use of these words after the general entries. Proverbs are often learned as whole expressions. Make sure you understand the meaning of the whole short sentence before you use it.

(b) A **simile** is an expression we use to say someone or something is like something else. Similes usually include the words 'like' or 'as'. An example is *He has an appetite like a horse*. In other words, he eats a great deal. We also say *Her hands were as cold as ice* to express just how cold someone's hands were.

(c) A **metaphor** is a more complicated construction than a simile or a proverb. A metaphor describes something by referring to something else. You give something a quality or a characteristic by calling it something else. You do not use the words 'like' or 'as'. Instead, for instance, you might say that a very shy, quiet or timid person is *such a mouse*. Here are some other examples:

I think what this committee should do is **clear the air** *before we move on to the major issues to be discussed today.*

clear the air = sort out differences, problematic areas/behaviour/matters;

She remembered the day she twisted her ankle. It was a **blessing in disguise**. *She had not been able to play netball for the whole term, but that meant she had had time for her studies. She would never have got an A for English otherwise.*

blessing in disguise = something problematic later becomes positive.

Idiomatic expressions are often included in dictionary entries after the more standard meanings of the word. Note that there may be a number of idiomatic uses of the same word: e.g. **cut** can be used idiomatically in a number of ways: **to cut a long story short** = you say you will 'cut a long story short' so that you can give someone a brief or condensed version of a long or rambling story;

to cut someone dead = to ignore them, not see them, or walk past them when you already know them.

to cut someone short = to interrupt someone and prevent them continuing.

(There are several other idiomatic uses of 'cut'.)

Here are some idiomatic expressions you may come across:

be born yesterday = to be innocent, unexposed to the world or to a issue
be left out in the cold = to be ignored by a group of people
catch someone's eye = to be noticed by someone
get the chop = to be fired from a job/position, to be killed
climb down = to admit you are wrong
costs the earth = something is very expensive
a drop in the ocean = a very small amount/contribution
be at the end of one's tether = to be desperate, unable to go on
a flash in the pan = a sudden/unexpected success
fly off the handle = to lose one's temper
go round in circles = to not get to the point, have no direction
good for nothing = useless
have your heart in the right place = to mean well
a house of cards = a plan which can easily be destroyed
a household name = someone famous
jump the gun = to do something before you should
keep at it = to work hard at something
kick someone when they're down = add to a person's difficulties
knock something = to criticize it
let the cat out of the bag = to release information, to reveal something
be in the limelight = to be famous
live beyond your means = not to have enough money to pay your way
lock, stock and barrel = everything
make a killing = to make a huge profit
make a mountain out of a molehill = make too much out of something
make headway = proceed, make progress
a mixed blessing = partly favourable, partly not
next to nothing = very little
open and shut = quite clear
out of the blue = sudden
over your head = too difficult, beyond your understanding
overstep the mark = to go too far
pass the buck = pass on the blame/responsibility to another
pay lip service = to support/agree without believing
in the pipeline = being completed or prepared
play with fire = to take risks
powers that be = authorities
pull your weight = to perform your role/contribution well
race the clock = to try to finish something within a set time
rank and file = ordinary people
read between the lines = to work out what's not said but suggested
red tape = bureaucracy

ride high = to have been successful

risk your neck = to take a great risk

race the clock = to try to finish something within a set time

save face = avoid losing status, avoid humiliation

set someone's mind at rest = to reassure them

show your face = to turn up, appear

sit tight = to keep your position, wait, not act

a slap on the back = praise

stand your ground = to be firm

take heart = to be encouraged

take pains = to go to considerable effort

think twice = to think over something again

turn a blind eye = to pretend not to see

up and coming = a person who is going to be successful

a vicious circle = something that eventually leads back to where it started

win the day = succeed in the long run

(d) Clichés

Many proverbs, similes and metaphors are useful. However, some of them are used more often than others and, as a result, become stale. You should avoid the ones which you always seem to read and hear. Expressions which are over-used are called **clichés**. For example, if you respond to someone's unhappiness by saying "It will get worse before it gets better," you are responding to the situation with a cliché, a stereotypic expression. Keep a look out for them and when you are going to use an idiomatic expression, first ask yourself if you could put what you want to say into your own words.

7 Writing skills

Most of your work in school and college will be written in English. Good writers always check what they have written. They look out for grammatical errors, to see if words have been spelt correctly, to check that words have been used appropriately and, most importantly, to make sure that the meaning is clear. In other words, good writers are their own editors.

You need to make sure that you have said what you wanted to and that you have said it with an accurate use of language structures and functions. You also need to be sure that you have produced clear paragraphs and that your ideas and points can be followed easily.

There are a number of things which you can do to check your work. These are covered below.

(a) Punctuation

Punctuation exists to help us break up written language into meaningful parts. We do this in sentences, within sentences and in paragraphs.

(i) The sentence

The sentence is a unit of meaning. It contains a point or idea that can be expressed within one grammatical piece. A sentence begins with a capital letter and closes with a full stop. A sentence can be punctuated in a number of ways depending on the construction of the sentence. These points of punctuation are covered below.

(ii) The full stop [.]
The full stop is used to—

1. mark the end of a sentence. This should be where the point/idea comes to a close. The sentence should consist of a main clause with a stop at the end or a main clause and supporting clause(s) followed by a stop;
2. indicate abbreviations: e.g. Post Office = P.O. Abbreviated words which end in the last letter of the word, for example Doctor = Dr do not have a stop after the last letter. However, abbreviations which do not end in the last letter of the word do have a stop: e.g. Hospital = hosp. Note that some abbreviations are taken from the Latin: for example (e.g.) is taken from *exempli gratia* and N.B. from the Latin *nota bene* (mark well).
3. indicate something is missing or words have been deliberately left out: e.g. *He said . . . and the police would . . .*
4. show something is fading out: e.g. *He said he would go but . . .*

(iii) The comma [,]
The comma is used to—

1. break the main clause from the clause which supports the main clause;
2. break phrases which contain additional information: *Let's go to the gallery on Saturday, it will be a lovely thing to do.;*
3. separate clauses divided by: and, but, or, nor, for;
4. separate adjectives after a noun e.g. *The man was short, squat and talkative,* but *A tall graceful building* with no commas before the noun separating colour adjectives before the noun;
5. mark introductory phrases or words that introduce e.g. *In addition, he bought a tractor.*
6. list things: e.g. *potatoes, rice, beans, peas;*
7. indicate direct speech: *He said, "I must go to the gallery."*

(iv) The semi-colon [;]
The semi-colon is used to—

1. to divide up a sentence which has two main clauses but which the writer wants to connect but not divide into separate sentences: e.g. *. . . To err is human; to forgive divine.*
2. list clauses which refer back to the same subject: e.g. *She said they would purchase the necessary seeds; plant and water them; spray them with chemicals; and check on them.*

(v) The colon [:]
The colon can be used to—

1. list things: e.g. *They had bought everything they needed: bandages, plaster, antiseptic, scissors;*
2. introduce a quotation: e.g. *I would like to quote from her latest book: "An animal fights from instinct . . .";*

3. introduce an explanation: e.g. *Before I go further let me explain: pull the plant gently from . . .;*

4. mark a logical connection not stated: e.g. *My circumstances changed: I had married . . .;*

5. balance two comparisons or contrasts: e.g. *The river rose up: the bridge fell in . . .*

(vi) The question mark [?]

The question mark is used to—

1. show a direct question:
Have you understood why I am annoyed with you?

2. It ends a sentence beginning with a question word: e.g. *Why?*

• Do not use a question mark in reported or indirect speech:
e.g. *She asked why he was unhelpful.*

• Do not use a question mark in sentences in which there are questions within a sentence which do not start with a question word:
She asked had I seen it and I said I hadn't.

(vii) The exclamation mark [!]

The exclamation mark is used for emphasis: e.g. *Get out! Hey!*

(viii) Quotation marks [' ' " "]

These are used to—

1. introduce a quotation: *The President said, "Zimbabwe is free."*

2. show a word has been taken from another text

3. to indicate the title of a poem, etc: *the review said that the poem, "The Morning After"* . . . (Note that titles of books and magazines are put in italics.)

4. suggest that the writer does not approve of the term: *They were talking about the 'natives'.*

(ix) The apostrophe [']

The apostrophe is used to indicate—

1. possession: *The child's toy,* i.e. the toy belonging to the child.

2. something has been left out: *It's* instead of *it is.*

(Remember not to confuse *it's* with the possessive pronoun *its* e.g. its roof.) N.B.: 1980s not 1980's.

(x) The dash [– —]

The dash is used to—

1. show a related but slightly different point when the writer does not want to interrupt the main part of the sentence;

2. mark off a summary of what has gone before it;

3. mark off a list from the main clause;

4. show a shift in the writing;

• The dash is used in more informal writing like personal letters where it can replace the colon, semi-colon, or brackets.

(xi) The hyphen [-]

The hyphen is used to—

1. make compound words, though some compound words in common use are no longer hyphenated;

2. where verbs and nouns are joined;

3. distinguish between different words with different forms.

(xii) **Brackets [( )]**

Brackets can be used

1. to denote information in 'parenthesis':

I bought a book ($10) and some cards ($1,50).

2. instead of commas or dashes when giving extra information:

I met her mother (Mrs Mamutse) at the shop.

(xiii) **Capital letters**

Capital letters are used to—

1. start a new sentence;

2. for proper nouns.

(b) **Style**

It is important that you choose the right level of formality or informality in your writing. Ask yourself:

Who will be reading what I am writing?

What is my relationship with that person?

If I am summarizing material, have I used my own words?

Am I expected to present the views of other writers?

Am I expected to present my own views?

How formal should the language be?

Can I use informal expressions?

(c) **Editing work**

When writing essays you should produce a first draft. This is a rough version of the essay. You should then read, correct, change and rewrite your essay. There are number of tips which might help you to be a more effective writer. Ask yourself the following questions for essays and summaries:

Do I understand what the **question** is asking me to do?

Have I answered the question?

Have I answered all parts of the question?

Do I have a clear **introduction** which sets out the things the essay covers?

What is my reader likely to think when s/he reads my introduction?

Does the essay have clear **paragraphs**?

Does each paragraph deal with one main point?

Do the paragraphs connect with each other?

Are any of the **sentences** too long?

Do I need to write shorter sentences?

Are all the **words** I have used appropriate for the topic?

Have I checked the spelling of words I usually spell incorrectly?

Have I checked the spelling of new words?

If I have used specialist terms have I used them correctly?

Have I used my own words as far as possible?

Are there any words I have taken from the original piece of writing?
Have I covered all the **main points** in my summary/essay?
Have I **punctuated** my writing properly?
Have I used language **structures** accurately?
Are there any structures I usually get wrong and should check?

Have I written a **conclusion**?
Is my conclusion clear and does it bring what I say to a close?
Is my handwriting clear?
Have I **checked** through the final copy before handing it in?

Perhaps you could read a friend's essay or summary and let your friend read yours. See what you notice about each other's written work. Is it what you would have noticed about your own? Can you make any further changes to your own work now?

8 Speaking skills – Communicating with people

When communicating with people we need to make sure that we speak when it is appropriate to speak, and listen when it is appropriate to listen. You should always try to say what it is you want to communicate using **short sentences** and words **appropriate** to the topic.

You should think about who you are talking to. You should think about how polite you should be, how much respect you need to show to the other person(s) and how formal or informal you can be. You should always try to speak clearly and audibly. If you mumble or speak with your fingers or your pen in your mouth, people will find it difficult to hear or understand you and, if you are chewing gum, they will think that you are rude.

Give other people a chance to reply to what you are saying, and also remember that it is important that you reply to them or comment on what they have been saying.

One of the sections above is concerned with language functions. Here are several more which might be useful in conversation. Remember that there are many ways in which you can perform these functions, so do not learn the examples below. Instead, see if you can think of ways of saying roughly the same things. Make a list of other language functions you use in your day-to-day life and think of formal and informal ways of saying them.

Note: informal speech often uses (a) short forms such as *I'll* instead of *I will*, *can't* instead of *cannot*, etc; (b) figurative language e.g. *I'm at my wits end, if you were in my shoes*, etc and (c) colloquialisms such as *Hi!* instead of *How do you do*, *OK* instead of *all right*, etc.

(a) **Starting conversations**

1. Introducing people (formal)—
   Mr Hove, I'd like you to meet Mr Chikowore. or
   Mr Hove, I'd like to introduce you to Mr Chikowore. (formal)
   Rufaro, this is/meet Tsitsi. (informal)

2. Meeting someone for the first time—

How do you do? I'm pleased to meet you. (formal)

Hello. How are you? (informal)

3. Using the telephone—

Good afternoon. May I please speak to Mrs Sibanda? My name is John Chiramba. I'm from Readwell Books. (formal)

Hello, Jenny. How are you? (informal)

(b) Ending conversations

1. Thanking and leaving—

Thank you very much for inviting us. We enjoyed meeting you. (formal)

Thanks for asking us round – we had a good time. (informal)

2. Saying goodbye—

It has been very good to have the opportunity to discuss the matter with you. We shall look forward to meeting again. (formal)

Thanks. We should go now. See you later / soon. (informal)

3. Ending a telephone conversation—

I am pleased I was able to reach you, Miss Mukombwe. I will look forward to seeing you on Tuesday. Goodbye. (formal)

I must go now, Tsitsi. I'll call you again later. Bye. (informal)

(c) Expressing opinions and values

1. Saying how sure or unsure you are—

I am quite certain that there will be no problem with your booking. (formal)

Look, Mercy, there's really no need for you to worry. (informal)

We are a little concerned about the figures in the second table. Would you mind explaining them to us? (formal)

I just don't know the answer, Brian. I don't know what to do and I am at my wits' end. (informal)

2. Asking for an opinion—

Mr Thomas, what is your view of the housing shortage? (formal)

Janey, what do you think of this one, it's cheap? (informal)

3. Giving an opinion—

In our considered opinion the strike is illegal. (formal)

I think the workers have a really good case. (informal)

4. Agreeing with an opinion—

We are in total agreement with the position that you have taken. (formal)

Yes, I think you're right. (informal)

5. Disagreeing with an opinion—

We are not certain that your account of the incident is accurate. (formal)

I can't believe that's what you really think. (informal)

(d) Asking for advice and giving advice

1. Asking for advice—
   Perhaps you could advise us what to do with this particular problem.
   (formal)
   What would you do if you were in my shoes? (informal)

2. Giving advice—
   I would recommend that you avoid eating chocolate altogether.
   (formal)
   If I were you, lay off the chocolates! (informal)

APPENDIX I

Words ending in -able and -ible

The use of **-able** or **-ible** at the end of a word is something which often causes problems, and even authorities on the English language do not always agree on whether a word should end in **-able** or **-ible**. The lists given here are a guide to commons words which must always end in **-able** and words which must always end in **-ible**.

-able		*-ible*	
advisable	manageable	accessible	indefensible
agreeable	measurable	admissible	indelible
ascribable	moveable	audible	indigestible
atonable	noticeable	avertible	incorruptible
baptizable	palatable	collapsible	incredible
believable	pleasurable	comprehensible	indigestible
confinable	preferable	controvertible	inflexible
conversable	readable	credible	intangible
creatable	receivable	discernible	intelligible
debatable	referable	divisible	irresistible
dissolvable	regrettable	edible	legible
endorsable	removable	eligible	neglible
forgivable	saleable	expressible	ostensible
immovable	serviceable	feasible	permissible
inflatable	sizable	flexible	plausible
irreconcilable	solvable	gullible	reducible
lapsable	tameable	incomprehensible	reprehensible
laughable	unmistakable	incorruptible	tangible
lovable	unshakable	incredible	visible
malleable	usable		

Use of -ise and -ize

There is a tendency in modern English to use **-ize** in most cases, but there are some words, given in the list here, that must end in **-ise**:

advertise	devise	otherwise
advise	disguise	premise
apprise *(to inform)*	enterprise	prise *(to prise open)*
chastise	excise	reprise
circumcise	exercise	supervise
comprise	franchise	surmise
compromise	improvise	surprise
demise	incise	televise
despise	merchandise	treatise

PART FIVE

General Knowledge

Universal Declaration of Human Rights

On 10 December, 1948, the General Assembly of the United Nations adopted and proclaimed the Universal Declaration of Human Rights, one of the most important international documents to have been agreed, which remains the basis for all international and national debate about our rights. Here is the full text of this historic document.

PREAMBLE

Whereas recognition of the inherent dignity and of the equal and inalienable rights of all members of the human family is the foundation of freedom, justice and peace in the world.

Whereas disregard and contempt for human rights have resulted in barbarous acts which have outraged the conscience of mankind, and the advent of a world in which human beings shall enjoy freedom of speech and belief and freedom from fear and want has been proclaimed as the highest aspiration of the common people.

Whereas it is essential, if man is not to be compelled to have recourse, as a last resort, to rebellion against tyranny and oppression, that human rights should be protected by the rule of law.

Whereas it is essential to promote the development of friendly relations between nations.

Whereas the people of the United Nations have in the Charter reaffirmed their faith in fundamental human rights, in the dignity and worth of the human person and in the equal rights of men and women and have determined to promote social progress and better standards of life in larger freedom.

Wheareas Member States have pledged themselves to achieve, in co-operation with the United Nations, the promotion of universal respect for and observance of human rights and fundamental freedom.

Whereas a common understanding of these rights and freedoms is of the greatest importance for the full realization of this pledge.

Now, Therefore,

THE GENERAL ASSEMBLY

proclaims

THIS UNIVERSAL DECLARATION OF HUMAN RIGHTS as a common standard of achievement for all peoples and all nations, to the end that every individual and every organ of society, keeping this Declaration constantly in mind, shall strive by teaching and education to promote respect for these rights and freedoms and by progressive measures, national and international, to secure their universal and effective recognition and observance, both among the peoples of Member States themselves and among peoples of territories under their jurisdiction.

Article 1. All human beings are born free and equal in dignity and rights. They are endowed with reason and conscience and should act towards one another in a spirit of brotherhood.

Article 2. Everyone is entitled to all the rights and freedoms set forth in this Declaration, without distinction of any kind, such as race, colour, sex, language, religion, political or other opinion, national or social origin, property, birth or other status.

Furthermore, no distinction shall be made on the basis of the political, jurisdictional or international status of the country or territory to which a person belongs, whether it be independent, trust, non-self-governing or under any other limitation of sovereignty.

Article 3. Everyone has the right to life, liberty and security of person.

Article 4. No one shall be held in slavery or servitude; slavery and the slave trade shall be prohibited in all their forms.

Article 5. No one shall be subjected to torture or to cruel, inhuman or degrading treatment or punishment.

Article 6. Everyone has the right to recognition everywhere as a person before the law.

Article 7. All are equal before the law and are entitled without any discrimination to equal protection of the law. All are entitled to equal protection against any discrimination in violation of this Declaration and against any incitement to such discrimination.

Article 8. Everyone has the right to an effective remedy by the competent national tribunals for acts violating the fundamental rights granted him by the constitution or by law.

Article 9. No one shall be subjected to arbitary arrest, detention or exile.

Article 10. Everyone is entitled in full equality to a fair and public hearing by an independent and impartial tribunal, in the determination of his rights and obligations and of any criminal charge against him.

Article 11. (1) Everyone charged with a penal offence has the right to be presumed innocent until proved guilty according to law in a public trial at which he has had all the guarantees necessary for his defence.

(2) No one shall be held guilty of any penal offence on account of any act or omission which did not constitute a penal offence, under national or international law, at a time when it was committed. Nor shall a heavier penalty be imposed than the one that was applicable at the time the penal offence was committed.

Article 12. No one shall be subjected to arbitary interference with his privacy, family, home or correspondence, nor to attacks upon his honour and reputation. Everyone has the right to the protection of the law against such interference or attacks.

Article 13. (1) Everone has the right to freedom of movement and residence within the borders of each state.

(2) Everyone has the right to leave any country, including his own, and to return to his country.

Article 14. (1) Everyone has the right to seek and to enjoy in other countries asylum from persecution.

(2) This right may not be invoked in the case of prosecutions genuinely

arising from non-political crimes or from acts contrary to the purposes and principles of the United Nations.

Article 15.(1) Everyone has the right to a nationality.

(2) No one shall be arbitrarily deprived of his nationality nor denied the right to change his nationality.

Article 16.(1) Men and women of full age, without any limitation due to race, nationality or religion, have the right to marry and to found a family. They are entitled to equal rights as to marriage, during marriage and at its dissolution.

(2) Marriage shall be entered into only with the free and full consent of the intending spouses.

(3) The family is the natural and fundamental group unit of society and is entitled to protection by society and the state.

Article 17.(1) Everyone has the right to own property alone as well as in association with others.

(2) No one shall be arbitrarily deprived of his property.

Article 18. Everyone has the right to freedom of thought, conscience and religion; this right includes freedom to change his religion or belief, and freedom, either alone or in community with others and in public or private, to manifest his religion or belief in teaching, practice, worship and observance.

Article 19. Everyone has the right to freedom of opinions and expression; this right includes freedom to hold opinions without interference and to seek, receive and impart information and ideas through any media and regardless of frontiers.

Article 20. (1) Everyone has the right to freedom of peaceful assembly and association.

(2) No one may be compelled to belong to an association.

Article 21.(1) Everyone has the right to take part in the government of his country, directly or through freely chosen representatives.

(2) Everyone has the right of equal access to public service in his country.

(3) The will of the people shall be the basis of the authority of government; this will shall be expressed in periodical and genuine elections which shall be by universal and equal suffrage and shall be held by secret vote or by equivalent free voting procedures.

Article 22. Everyone, as a member of society, has the right to social security and is entitled to realization, through national effort and international co-operation and in accordance with the organization and resources of each State, of the economic, social and cultural rights indispensable for his dignity and the free development of his personality.

Article 23. (1) Everyone has the right to work, to free choice of employment, to just and favourable conditions of work and to protection against unemployment.

(2) Everyone, without any discrimination, has the right to equal pay for equal work.

(3) Everyone who works has the right to just and favourable remuneration ensuring for himself and his family an existance worthy of human dignity, and supplemented, if necessary, by other means of social protection.

(4) Everyone has the right to form and to join trade unions for the protection of his interests.

Article 24. Everyone has the right to rest and leisure, including reasonable limitation of working hours and periodic holidays with pay.

Article 25. (1) Everyone has the right to a standard of living adequate for the health and well-being of himself and of his family, including food, clothing, housing and medical care and necessary social services, and the right to security in the event of unemployment, sickness, disability, widowhood, old age or other lack of livelihood in circumstances beyond his control.

(2) Motherhood and childhood are entitled to special care and assistance. All children, whether born in or out of wedlock, shall enjoy the same social protection.

Article 26. (1) Everyone has the right to education. Education shall be free, at least in the elementary and fundamental stages. Elementary education shall be compulsory. Technical and professional education shall be made generally available and higher education shall be equally accessible to all on the basis of merit.

(2) Education shall be directed to the full development of the human personality and to the strengthening of respect for human rights and fundamental freedoms. It shall promote understanding, tolerance and friendship among all nations, racial and religious groups, and shall further the activities of the United Nations for the maintenance of peace.

(3) Parents have a prior right to choose the kind of education that shall be given to their children.

Article 27. (1) Everyone has the right freely to participate in the cultural life of the community, to enjoy the arts and to share in scientific advancement and its benefits.

(2) Everyone has the right to the protection of the moral and material interests resulting from any scientific, literary or artistic production of which he is the author.

Article 28. Everyone is entitled to a social and international order in which the rights and freedoms set forth in this Declaration can be fully realized.

Article 29. (1) Everyone has duties to the community in which alone the free and full development of his personality is possible.

(2) In the exercise of his rights and freedoms, everyone shall be subject to such limitations as are determined by law solely for the purpose of securing due recognition and respect for the rights and freedoms of others and of meeting the just requirements of morality, public order and the general welfare in a democratic society.

(3) These rights and freedoms may in no case be exercised contrary to the purposes and principles of the United Nations.

Article 30. Nothing in this Declaration may be interpreted as implying for any State, group or person any right to engage in any activity or to perform any act aimed at the destruction of any of the rights and freedoms set forth herein.

THE SOLAR SYSTEM

The solar system is made up of the sun, the planets and their moons. Listed here is each planet, beginning with the planet nearest the sun and ending with the planet farthest away from the sun. Alongside each planet is its distance from the sun, its diameter, its temperature and the number of moons which orbit around it.

Planet	Distance	Diameter	Temperature	Moons
Mercury	57 900 000km	4 878km	−193°C to 342°C	none
Venus	108 200 000km	12 100km	−455°C	none
Earth	149 600 000km	12 756km	−88,29 to 58°C	1
Mars	228 000 000km	6 790km	−124°C to −31°C	2
Jupiter	778 400 000km	142 700km	−149°C	16
Saturn	1 424 600 000km	120 000km	−176°C	over 20
Uranus	2 866 900 000km	50 800km	−216°C	5
Neptune	4 486 100 000km	48 600km	−218°C	2
Pluto	5 890 000 000km	3 000km	−184°C	1

Each planet orbits around the sun. Those nearest the sun take a shorter time to complete their orbits than those farthest away from the sun. They also differ in the length of time they take to turn on their own axis. The time taken by each planet to complete its orbit and to turn on its axis is given here.

Mercury	88 days	59 days
Venus	225 days	243 days
Earth	365 days	23 hours 56 minutes
Mars	687 days	24 hours 37 minutes
Jupiter	11,9 years	9 hours 50 minutes
Saturn	29,5 years	10 hours 14 minutes
Uranus	84 years	probably 16 hours
Neptune	165 years	probably 18 hours 24 mins
Pluto	248 years	probably 153 hours

The list given here shows the gases of which each planet is composed.

Mercury	helium, hydrogen, oxygen
Venus	carbon dioxide, nitrogen, helium, neon, argon, water vapour, sulphur, carbon, oxygen
Earth	nitrogen, oxygen, carbon dioxide, water vapour
Mars	carbon dioxide, nitrogen, oxygen, argon, carbon monoxide, neon, krypton, xenon, water vapour
Jupiter	hydrogen, helium, methane, ammonia, ethane, acetylene, phosphine, water vapour, carbon monoxide
Saturn	hydrogen, helium, methane, ammonia, ethane, phosphine
Uranus	hydrogen, helium, methane
Neptune	hydrogen, helium, methane, ethane
Pluto	methane, and possibly ammonia and water

Constellations

The Milky Way galaxy in which our solar system lies contains about 100 000 million stars. Scientists have grouped those stars we can see from the earth into 80 constellations and given each constellation a name. Twelve constellations were named by the Ancient Greeks and are known as the Signs of the Zodiac (the word 'zodiac' was the name given by the Greeks to the part of the sky with which they were familiar).

The list here gives the names of all constellations; those that are in italics are the Signs of the Zodiac.

Andromeda	Crux	Pavo
Apus	Cygnus	Pegasus
Ara	Delphinus	Perseus
Aries	Dorado	Phoenix
Aquarius	Draco	Pictor
Aquila	Eridanus	*Pisces*
Auriga	Equuleus	Piscis Austrinus
Bootes	Fornax	Puppis
Camelopardalis	*Gemini*	Pyxis
Cancer	Grus	Reticulum
Canes Venatici	Hercules	Sagitta
Canis Major	Hydra	*Sagittarius*
Canis Minor	Hydrus	*Scorpio*
Capricornus	Indus	Sculptor
Carina	Lacerta	Serpens
Cassiopeia	*Leo*	Sextans
Centaurus	Leo minor	*Taurus*
Cepheus	Lepus	Telescopium
Cetus	*Libra*	Triangulum
Chamaeleon	Lupus	Triangulum Australe
Circinus	Lynx	Tucana
Columba	Lyra	Ursa Major
Coma Berenices	Monoceros	Ursa Minor
Corona Australis	Musca	Vela
Corona Borealis	Octans	*Virgo*
Corvus	Ophiuchus	Volans
Crater	Orion	

Signs of the Zodiac

Aquarius (the water bearer) - January 21 - February 19
Pisces (the fish) - February 20 - March 20
Aries (the ram) - March 21 to April 20
Taurus (the bull) - April 21 to May 20
Gemini (the twins) - May 21 to June 21
Cancer (the crab) - June 22 to July 23
Leo (the Lion) - July 24 to August 23
Virgo (the virgin) - August 24 to September 23
Libra (the scales) - September 24 to October 23
Scorpio (the scorpion) - October 24 to November 22
Sagittarius (the centaur) - November 23 to December 22
Capricorn (the goat) - December 23 to January 20

THE EARTH

About 71% of the Earth's surface is water. Only 29% is land. The composition of the Earth – rocks, soils, water, plants and animals – has taken more than 4 700 million years to evolve.

The time from the beginning of the Earth to the present has been divided by scientists into eras, which in turn are divided into ages and these in turn are divided into periods. This division is known as the Geological Time Scale.

Geological Time Scale
(with Ages given in millions of years)

Era	Age	Period	Conditions
Azoic Proterozoic	4 700 3 000	Pre-Cambrian	Barren landscapes; heavy rains several ice ages; life begins
Palaeozoic (ancient life)	570	Cambrian	Shallow seas; some volcanoes; warm climate
	500	Ordovician	Seas retreat and advance; volcanic activity; warm climate; first animals with back bones
	440	Silurian	Sea-level rises and falls; some mountains formed; land plants appear
	395	Devonian	Mountain building in northern hemisphere; plants and fishes abundant; amphibians appear
	345	Carboniferous	Shallow seas and swamps; large insects and first reptiles; trees up to 30m high
	280	Permian	High mountains formed; deserts in northern hemisphere
Mesozoic	225	Triassic	Shallow seas, salt lakes and deserts; first dinosaurs and mammals
	195	Jurassic	Sea invades land; continents (middle life) begin to drift apart; reptiles evolve; dinosaurs prevalent
	136	Cretaceous	Swamps; mountain building; spread of flowering plants and insects
Cainozoic (recent life)	65	Palaeocene	Sea advances; warm climate; dinosaurs and other reptiles extinct
	54	Eocene	Mountain building; some volcanic activity; warm climate; beginning of modern mammals
	38	Oligocene	Mountain building; warm climate; grasslands; mammals spread
	26	Miocene	Mountain building; appearance of primitive ape
	7	Pliocene	Climate like present climate; land similar to today; manlike apes evolving
	2	Pleistocene	Ice sheets advance in northern hemisphere; development of primitive man
50 000BC		Holocene	Ice retreats; rise of sea level; forests develop; man becomes dominant animal

Time zones

The Earth turns on its own axis through 360° every 24 hours. The world is divided into 24 time zones. Each span of 15° longitude represents 1 hour. The longitude 0° passes through Greenwich, which is part of London in England and is known as the Greenwich meridian. The 15° intervals are measured from this line.

Zimbabwe lies 30° East of the Greenwich meridian. Therefore it is 2 hours ahead of Greenwich. Thus if you want to telephone someone in London during lunch hour, you must wait until 3 o'clock Zimbabwe time, when it will be 1 o'clock London time.

Sydney in Australia is 150° East of Greenwich and 120° East of Zimbabwe. Therefore it is 8 hours ahead of Zimbabwe. If you want to watch a tennis match in Australia being transmitted live on television at 2 o'clock in the afternoon Australian time, you would have to turn on your television in Zimbabwe at 6 o'clock in the morning.

Parallels of latitude

There are five main parallels of latitude:

The Equator	0°
The Tropic of Cancer	23 and a half ° north of the Equator
The Tropic of Capricorn	23 and a half ° south of the Equator
The Arctic Circle	66 and a half ° north of the Equator
The Antarctic Circle	66 and a half ° south of the Equator

ANIMALS AND PLANTS

Animals (fauna) and plants (flora) are classified by scientists into a hierarchy. At the top of the hierarchy are five kingdoms, namely: Plants, Animals, Fungi (moulds, mushrooms, toadstools, etc), Protista (single-celled organisms) and Monera (bacteria and related organisms). At the bottom of the hierarchy are species.

A kingdom is divided into phyla (singular: phylum). A phylum is divided into classes. A class is divided into orders. An order is divided into families. A family is divided into genera (singular: genus). And a genus is divided into species.

To illustrate this classification take the example of a common animal, the domestic dog, and a common Zimbabwean tree, the musasa, *Brachystegia spiciformes*, and move up through the hierarchy.

Species	*Canis familiaris*		*Brachystegia spiciformes*
Genus	*Canis*		*Brachystegia*
Family	Canidae		Fabaceae
Order	Carnivora	(carnivores)	Fabales
Class	Mammalia	(mammals)	Angiospermae
Phylum	Chordata	(vertebrates)	Tracheophyta
Kingdom	Animalia		Plantae

There are twelve phyla in the animal kingdom. These phyla, and the animals they contain, are given here, ranging from the most primitive forms to the most advanced animals.

Protozoa	single celled organisms
Parazoa	sponges
Coelenterata	jellyfish, sea anemones, corals
Platyhelminthes	flatworms, flukes, tapeworms
Aschelminthes	roundworms, animacules
Polyzoa	moss animals
Brachiopoda	lamp shells
Mollusca	oysters, snails, mussels, etc
Annelida	earthworms, leeches, etc
Arthropoda	insects, crabs, spiders, scorpions, etc
Echinodermata	starfishes, sea urchins, etc
Chordata	reptiles, fishes, birds, mammals (including man)

CHEMICAL SYMBOLS

The list here gives all the known chemicals in the world and the symbols by which they are recognized.

Actinium	Ac	Helium	He	Promethium	Pm
Aluminium	Al	Holmium	Ho	Protactinium	Pa
Antimony	Sb	Hydrogen	H	Radium	Ra
Argon	Ar	Indium	In	Radon	Rn
Arsenic	As	Iodine	I	Rhenium	Re
Astatine	At	Iridium	Ir	Rhodium	Rh
Barium	Ba	Iron	Fe	Rubidium	Rb
Berkelium	Bk	Krypton	Kr	Samarium	Sm
Bismuth	Bi	Lanthanum	La	Scandium	Sc
Boron	B	Lawrencium	Lr	Selenium	Se
Bromine	Br	Lead	Pb	Silicon	Si
Cadmium	Cd	Lithium	Li	Silver	Ag
Calcium	Ca	Lutetium	Lu	Sodium	Na
Californium	Cf	Magnesium	Mg	Strontium	Sr
Carbon	C	Manganese	Mn	Sulphur	S
Cerium	Ce	Mandelevium	Md	Tantalum	Ta
Cesium	Cs	Mercury	Hg	Technetium	Tc
Chlorine	Cl	Molybdenum	Mo	Tellurium	Te
Chromium	Cr	Neodymium	Nd	Terbium	Tb
Cobalt	Co	Neon	Ne	Thallium	Tl
Copper	Cu	Neptunium	Np	Thorium	Th
Curium	Cm	Nickel	Ni	Thulium	Tm
Dysprosium	Dy	Niobium	Nb	Tin	Sn
Einsteinium	Es	Nitrogen	N	Titanium	Ti
Erbium	Er	Nobelium	No	Tungsten	W
Europium	Eu	Osmium	Os	Uranium	U
Fermium	Fm	Oxygen	O	Vanadium	V
Fluorine	F	Palladium	Pd	Xenon	Xe
Francium	Fr	Phosphorus	P	Ytterbium	Yb
Gadolinium	Gd	Platinum	Pt	Yttrium	Y
Gallium	Ga	Plutonium	Pu	Zinc	Zn
Germanium	Ge	Polonium	Po	Zirconium	Zr
Gold	Au	Potassium	K		
Hafnium	Hf	Praseodymium	Pr		

WEIGHTS AND MEASURES

Linear

km	kilometre	10 mm	=	1 cm
m	metre	10 cm	=	1 dm
dm	decimetre	10 dm	=	1 m
cm	centimetre	100 cm	=	1 m
mm	millimetre	1000 m	=	1 km

Conversions:

25,4 mm	=	1 inch
0,91 m	=	1 yard
1,83 m	=	1 fathom
1,61 km	=	1 mile

Weight

kg	kilogram	10 mg	=	1 cg
gm	gram	10 cg	=	1 dg
dg	decigram	10 dg	=	1 gm
cg	centigram	100 cg	=	1 gm
mg	milligram	1000 gm	=	1 kg

Conversions:

28 gm	=	1 ounce
0,45 kg	=	1 pound
1016 kg	=	1 ton
1000 kg	=	1 metric tonne (2 204 pounds)

Fluid

kl	kilolitre	10 ml	=	1 cl
l	litre	10 cl	=	1 dl
dl	decilitre	10 dl	=	1 l
cl	centilitre	100 cl	=	1 l
ml	millilitre	1000 l	=	1 kl
		1 l	=	1000 cubic cm
		1 000 l	=	1 cubic metre

Conversions:

0,57 l	=	1 pint
4,55 l	=	1 gallon
28 cu cm	=	1 fluid ounce

Square measure

100 sq mm	=	1 sq cm		*Conversions:*		
10 000 sq cm	=	1 sq m		0,84 sq m	=	1 square yard
1 000 000 sq m	=	1 sq km		2,59 sq km	=	1 square mile
1 sq m	=	1 centiare		0,4 hectares	=	1 acre
100 centiares	=	1 are				
100 ares	=	1 hectare				
100 hectares	=	1 sq km				

Temperature

In some countries temperature is measured in Celsius; in others it is measured in Fahrenheit. To convert Celsius to Fahrenheit, or vice versa, use these formulae:

$$C = x°F - 32 \times 5 \div 9 \qquad\qquad F = x°C + 32 \times 9 \div 5$$

MATHEMATICAL FORMULAE

Key			
a	= area	h	= height
b	= base	l	= length
br	= breadth	π	= 3,142
c	= circumference	r	= radius
d	= diameter	w	= width

Square
Area: $l \times br$
Perimeter: $l \times 4$
Side: $\sqrt{a}$

Rectangle
Area: $l \times br$
Length: $a + br$
Breadth: $a + l$
Perimeter: $2\,(l + br)$

Parallelogram and rhombus
Area: $br \times h$

Trapezium
Area:
$w + 2 \times$ (sum of parallel sides)

Triangle
Area: $(b \times h) + 2$
Height: $(a \times 2) + b$
Base: $(a \times 2) + h$

Circle
Circumference: $2\pi r$
Diameter: $c + \pi$
Radius: $c + 2\pi$
Area: πr^2

Cylinder
Area of curved surface: $2\pi r \times h$
Area of ends: $2\pi r^2$
Volume: $\pi r^2 h$

Cone
Area of curved surface:
$\pi r \times$ slant height
Area of total surface:
$(\pi r^2) + (\pi r \times$ slant height$)$

Volume: $(2\pi r^2) \times (h + 3)$

Sphere
Area: $4\,\pi r^2$
Volume: $4\pi r^2 + 3$

Cube
Area: $6 \times l^2$
Volume: $l \times br \times h$

Pyramid
Area of slant surface:
(perimeter of $b + 2$) $\times$ slant height
Area of total surface:
a of slant surface + a of b
Volume: $(a$ of $b + 3) \times h$

ROMAN NUMERALS

The numerals which we use commonly use 1 2 3 4 5 6 7 8 9 10, etc are known as Arabic numerals, because they derive from an Arabic system of counting. We also sometimes use Roman numerals. For example, you will see Roman numerals on some clock faces, after a person's name (Henry VIII), or to denote a year (credits for television features often carry the year the feature was made in Roman numerals).

Using the following list of Roman numerals you should be able to write any combination of numbers. For example, to work out the year of Zimbabwe's independence, 1980, add one thousand (M), nine hundred (CM) and eighty (LXXX). The year 1980 expressed in Roman numerals is therefore MCMLXXX.

1	I	11	XI	30	XXX	400	CCCC
2	II	12	XII	40	XL	500	D
3	III	13	XIII	50	L	600	DC
4	IV	14	XIV	60	XL	700	DCC
5	V	15	XV	70	LXX	800	DCCC
6	VI	16	XVI	80	LXXX	900	CM
7	VII	17	XVII	90	XC	1000	M
8	VIII	18	XVIII	100	C	2000	MM
9	IX	19	XIX	200	CC		
10	X	20	XX	300	CCC		

ROMAN AND GREEK GODS AND GODDESSES

Roman	Greek	Status
Jupiter	Zeus	King of all gods and god of thunder
Juno	Hera	Queen of heaven
Saturn	Cronos	God of time
Minerva	Pallas Athene	Goddess of wisdom and science
Vesta	Hestia	Goddess of fire
Apollo	Apollo	God of light, music, art and medicine
Diana	Artemis	Goddess of the woods, the hunt and the moon
Ceres	Demeter	Goddess of the fruits of the earth (crops)
Vulcan	Hephaestus	God of fire, iron, brass, gold and silver
Mercury	Hermes	God of travellers and merchants; messenger of the gods
Mars	Ares	God of war
Venus	Aphrodite	Goddess of love
Bacchus	Dionysus	God of wine
Themis	Artemis	Goddess of equity, law and peace
Cupid	Eros	God of love
Pan	Pan	God of shepherds and hunters
Pluto	Hades	God of the underworld
Uranus	Uranus	God of the heaven
Helius	Helios	God of the sun

In Greek mythology there were many other lesser gods. Some of the most well-known ones belonged to the groups listed here.

The Graces	Aglaia, Thalia and Euphrosyne, who bestowed grace, humour and good manners
The Muses	Clio, muse of history; Euterpe, muse of lyric poetry; Thalia, muse of comedy; Melpomene, muse of tragedy; Terpsichore, muse of dance; Erato, muse of love lyrics; Polyhymnia, muse of hymns; Urania, muse of astronomy; and Calliope, muse of epic poetry and eloquence
The Fates	Clotho, Lachesis and Atropos, three sisters who between them held the thread of life and cut it when the hour of fate struck

THE BIBLE

The Books of the Bible (with their contractions in brackets) are given here in the order in which appear in the Bible.

Old Testament

Genesis (Gen.)
Exodus (Exod.)
Leviticus (Lev.)
Numbers (Num.)
Deuteronomy (Deut.)
Joshua (Josh.)
Judges (Judg.)
Ruth (Ruth)
1 Samuel (1 Sam.)
2 Samuel (2 Sam.)
1 Kings
2 Kings
1 Chronicles (1 Chron.)
2 Chronicles (2 Chron.)
Ezra
Nehemiah (Neh.)
Esther
Job
Psalms (Ps.)
Proverbs (Prov.)

Ecclesiastes (Eccl.)
Song of Solomon (Song of Sol.)
Isaiah (Isa.)
Jeremiah (Jer.)
Lamentations (Lam.)
Ezekiel (Ezek.)
Daniel (Dan.)
Hosea (Hos.)
Joel
Amos
Obadiah (Obad.)
Jonah
Micah
Nahum
Habakkuk (Hab.)
Zephaniah (Zeph.)
Haggai (Hag.)
Zechariah (Zech.)
Malachi (Mal.)

New Testament

Matthew (Matt.)
Mark
Luke
John
Acts
Romans (Rom.)
1 Corinthians (1 Cor.)
2 Corinthians (2 Cor.)
Galatians (Gal.)
Ephesians (Eph.)
Philippians (Phil.)
Colossians (Col.)
1 Thessalonians (1 Thess.)
2 Thessalonians (2 Thess.)

1 Timothy (1 Tim.)
2 Timothy (2 Tim.)
Titus
Philemon (Philem.)
Hebrews (Heb.)
James (Jas.)
1 Peter (1 Pet.)
2 Peter (2 Pet.)
1 John
2 John
3 John
Jude
Revelation (Rev.)

Apocrypha

1 Esdras
2 Esdras
Tobit
Judith
Esther
Wisdom of Solomon (Wisd. of Sol.)
Ecclesiasticus (Ecclus.)
Baruch

Song of the Three Children (Song 3 Childr.)
Susanna
Bell & the Dragon (Bell & Dr.)
Prayer of Manasses (Pr. Manasses)
1 Maccabees (1 Macc.)
2 Maccabees (2 Macc.)

SHAKESPEARE'S WORKS
(with common abbreviations in parentheses)

The Comedies
All's Well that Ends Well (*All's Well*)
A Midsummer-Night's Dream (*Mids. N. D.*)
As You Like It (*A.Y.L.*)
Love's Labour's Lost (*L.L.L.*)
Measure for Measure (*Meas. for M.*)
Much Ado About Nothing (*Much Ado*)
The Comedy of Errors (*Com. Err.*)
The Merchant of Venice (*Merch. V.*)
The Merry Wives of Windsor (*Merry W.*)
The Taming of the Shrew (*Tam. Shr.*)
The Tempest (*Temp.*)
The Two Gentlemen of Verona (*Two Gent.*)
The Winter's Tale (*Wint. T.*)
Twelfth Night; or, What You Will (*Twel. N.*)

The Histories
The Life and Death of King John (*K. John*)
The Tragedy of King Richard II (*Rich. II*)
The First Part of King Henry IV (*1 Hen. IV*)
The Second Part of King Henry IV (*2 Hen. IV*)
The Life of King Henry V (*Hen. V*)
The First Part of King Henry VI (*1 Hen. VI*)
The Second Part of King Henry VI (*2 Hen. VI*)
The Third Part of King Henry VI (*3 Hen. VI*)
The Tragedy of King Richard III (*Rich III*)
The Famous History of the Life of King Henry VIII (*Hen. VIII*)

The Tragedies
Antony and Cleopatra (*Ant. & Cl.*)
King Lear (*Lear*)
Coriolanus (*Coriol.*)
Cymbeline (*Cymb.*)
Hamlet, Prince of Denmark (*Haml.*)
Julius Caesar (*Jul. Caes.*)
King Lear (*Lear*)
Macbeth (*Macb.*)
Othello, the Moor of Venice (*Oth.*)
Pericles, Prince of Tyre (*Per.*)
Romeo and Juliet (*Rom. & Jul.*)
Timon of Athens (*Timon*)
Titus Andronicus (*Tit. A.*)
Troilus and Cressida (*Tr. & Cr.*)

The Poems
A Lover's Complaint (*Compl.*)
Sonnets (*Sonn.*)
The Phoenix and the Turtle (*Phoenix*)
The Passionate Pilgrim (*Pilgr.*)
The Rape of Lucrece (*Lucr.*)
Venus and Adonis (*Ven. & Ad.*)

FOREIGN ALPHABETS

Greek alphabet			Russian			Hebrew	
Α	α	Alpha	А	а	As	א	Aleph
Β	β	Beta	Б	б	Buki	ב	Beth
Γ	γ	Gamma	В	в	Wjedi	ג	Gimel
Δ	δ	Delta	Г	г	Glagol	ד	Daleth
Ε	ε	Epsilon	Д	д	Dobro	ה	He
Ζ	ζ	Zeta	Е	е	Jehst	ו	Vau
Η	η	Eta	Ж	ж	Schiwete	ז	Zain
Θ	θ	Theta	З	з	Semlja	ח	Cheth
Ι	ι	Iota	И	и	Ische	ט	Teth
Κ	κ	Kappa	Й	й	Ische	י	Iod
Λ	λ	Lambda	І	і	I	כ	Caph
Μ	μ	Mu	К	к	Kako	ל	Lamed
Ν	ν	Nu	Л	л	Ljudi	מ	Mem
Ξ	ξ	Xi or Si	М	м	Muislete	נ	Nun
Ο	ο	Omicron	Н	н	Nasch	ס	Samech
Π	π	Pi	О	о	On	ע	Oin
Ρ	ρ	Rho	П	п	Pakoy	פ	Pe
Σ	σ ς	Sigma	Р	р	Rzui	צ	Tzadde
Τ	τ	Tau	С	с	Sslowo	ק	Koph
Υ	υ	Upsilon	Т	т	Twerdo	ר	Resh
Φ	φ	Phi	У	у	U	שׁ	Shin
Χ	χ	Chi	Ф	ф	Fert	שׂ	Sin
Ψ	ψ	Psi	Х	х	Chherr	ת	Tau
Ω	ω	Omega	Ц	ц	Zui		
			Ч	ч	Tscherw		
			Ш	ш	Schs		
			Щ	щ	Schtscha		
			Ы	ы	Jerui		
			Ь	ь	Jher		
			Э	э	E		
			Ю	ю	Ju		
			Я	я	Ja		

INTERNATIONAL ALPHABET

It is often necessary to spell words over long-distance communications such as radios and telephones. To ensure that the listener hears the letters correctly, international call signs are used. This is an internationally accepted code of communication.

A – Alpha
B – Bravo
C – Charlie
D – Delta
E – Echo
F – Foxtrot
G – Golf
H – Hotel
I – India
J – Juliet
K – Kilo
L – Lima
M – Mike
N – November
O – Oscar
P – Poppa
Q – Quebec
R – Romeo
S – Sierra
T – Tango
U – Uniform
V – Victor
W – Whisky
X – X-ray
Y – Yankee
Z – Zulu

SEVEN WONDERS OF THE ANCIENT WORLD

The Seven Wonders of the Ancient World are listed here. Of the seven, only the Pyramids of Egypt still stand substantially as they were built.

The Colossus of Rhodes

This statue about 30 metres high was built in honour of the sun god to commemorate the end of the seige of Rhodes in 304 BC. It was erected by the harbour in about 285 BC but collapsed during an earthquake in 225 BC.

The Hanging Gardens of Babylon

These roof gardens, irrigated by water from the Euphrates River, were built by King Nebuchadnezzar in about 600 BC.

The Mausoleum of Halicarnassus

This monumental tomb of King Mausoleus was built by his widow, Queen Artemisia. Mausoleus was the King of Anatolia in the 4th century BC. Fragments of his tomb are housed in the British Museum in London.

The Pharos of Alexandria

This lighthouse on the island of Pharos near Alexandria in Egypt was built for the Pharoah Ptolemy in about 280 BC. It was over 130 metres high and remained standing until the 12th century AD.

The Pyramids of Egypt

These pyramids are located along a 80 kilometre stretch of the River Nile, near the site of the ancient city of Memphis. Built by the Pharoahs, they date from 2686 BC to 2160 BC. The most famous ones are the pyramids of Khufu, Khafre and Menkaure.

The Statue of Zeus at Olympus

This statue, over 9 metres high and plated with gold and ivory, showed Zeus on a throne. It was made in about 430 BC by an Athenian sculptor, Phidias, and was destroyed in the 5th century AD.

The Temple of Artemis at Ephesus

This temple was famous for its great size (over 90 metres by 45 metres) and for the art that adorned it. Built in about 550 BC by King Croesus and rebuilt in 356 BC, it was later destroyed by the Goths.